THE ELITE
PRACTICE FORMULA

Dr. Carlo Biasucci

Published by Motivational Press, Inc.
1777 Aurora Road
Melbourne, Florida, 32935
www.MotivationalPress.com

Manufactured in the United States of America.

ISBN: 978-1-62865-381-6

CONTENTS

FOREWORD

FIVE GREAT TRUTHS 6

SECTION 1 YOUR PERSONAL PRISON 11

CHAPTER 1

THE SOLO PRACTICE TRAP 12

CHAPTER 2

THE SOLO PRACTICE MODEL IS DEAD 17

CHAPTER 3

WHO AM I, AND WHY SHOULD YOU CARE? 21

CHAPTER 4

FIGHT BACK AND GAIN CONTROL 27

CHAPTER 5

THE 4 FOUNDATIONS OF THE ELITE PRACTICE 30

SECTION 2 SYSTEMS 35

CHAPTER 6

THERE'S A SYSTEM FOR THAT 36

CHAPTER 7

A FAIRY TALE EXPERIENCE 41

CHAPTER 8

SYSTEMATIC PRACTICE GROWTH 45

SECTION 3 TRAINING 51

CHAPTER 9

BUILDING THE ULTIMATE TEAM 52

CHAPTER 10

DELIVER THE FAIRY TALE EXPERIENCE
WITH *CONSISTENCY* 58

SECTION 4 LEADERSHIP................................... **61**

CHAPTER 11
ADOPT A WINNING MINDSET 62
CHAPTER 12
NO CLEAR DIRECTION 66
CHAPTER 13
ACTIVELY GROWING THE BUSINESS CULTURE 69
CHAPTER 14
LEVERAGE = FREEDOM 73
CHAPTER 15
WHY YOUR PEOPLE WILL FOLLOW YOU 78

SECTION 5 MARKETING **83**

CHAPTER 16
GET OUT OF THE BUSINESS OF DENTISTRY............ 84
CHAPTER 17
LEARN HOW TO FISH 88
CHAPTER 18
THEY'LL BREAK YOUR DOOR DOWN
IF YOU LEARN THIS.................................... 90
CHAPTER 19
AUTOMATE YOUR MARKETING,
MULTIPLY YOUR BUSINESS............................ 96
CHAPTER 20
WHERE AND WHAT TO INVEST 102

SECTION 6 PUTTING IT ALL TOGETHER **107**

CHAPTER 21
YOUR IDEAL PRACTICE LIFE 108
CHAPTER 22
FINAL COMMENTS 115

CITATIONS...118

To my wife Ashlee, who has been by my side for more than 15 years, and is a constant inspirational force that allows me to chase my dreams. And for my daughter Allison who reminds me every day what matters in life. These two very special ladies are the reason I do what I do.

To my fellow professionals,

I have written this book with the sincere intention that it will help you reignite the passion that burned in you when you first entered professional school. I hope your love for the profession inspires the next generation.

FOREWORD

FIVE GREAT TRUTHS

by Dan S. Kennedy

I have been actively and intimately involved with the dental profession in the U.S. and Canada for over 35 years, directly influencing with innovative practice growth strategies, and as behind-scenes 'Consultant To The Consultants'. More than 15,000 dentists and other health care practice professionals have gone through my own Trainings, and more than a dozen leaders of the field have worked or now work with me as their consultant and coach. From this, I have determined a few key Great Truths about the dentists who create exceptionally successful and sustainable practices AND satisfying professional lives, versus the overwhelming majority who, instead, live as Thoreau characterized "lives of *quiet desperation.*"

I'll tell you about these Great Truths briefly, in a minute, but first a word about this book and its author, Dr. Carlo Biasucci. I'm afraid my long-in-tooth (pardon poor pun) years, experience, observing "idea promoters" come and go has made me *jaded.* I am rarely impressed. But my look into what Dr. Biasucci has done and continues to do with his practice *has* impressed. Unless you have a monster ego standing in your way, it is impossible not to be impressed. And I can assure you, there is much worthy of *your* attention, analysis and application. I happen to prize AUTONOMY above virtually everything else, and above all else, I am impressed with Dr. Biasucci's clarity about and commitment to autonomy as a practice owner. This book shows the way on this road few ever travel.

NOW, TO THE PROMISED GREAT TRUTHS:

First, a systems driven business is the only kind of business that can be scaled without scaling up stress on its owner and its staff (and often its customers) to intolerable levels. Dedication to locked in, locked down systems is what separates a bad job disguised as a business from real business ownership. Most dentists actually have jobs. You can own a business that works for you instead of a slave-master you work for.

I've a friend who, early in his adult life, had a job as a prison guard. He said it was eerily difficult to tell the inmates from the guards – the only real difference that the guards went home at night but came back and got locked back up every morning. It's hard to confront such a reality. When he did, he quit immediately. I'm certainly not going to suggest quitting dentistry! – but I will suggest quitting any way of practicing that embodies this uncomfortable, core reality.

Second, to the extent that a business involves humans, especially humans interacting with customers, systems for and true mastery of recruiting, training, motivation and effective enforcement of best practices are crucial. In practice, staff and patients are in constant interaction. As *that* goes, so goes your income, your referrals, your opportunity for autonomy. Most dentists act as if it should mostly take care of itself, because they issue paychecks, maybe pay bonuses, and spring for a 'pizza Friday' now and then. Of course, most dental offices are, bluntly, perpetually or frequently dysfunctional. And most dentists are stressed by and complain about their staffs. So a radically different thought process about this is called for.

Third, all exceptionally successful, profitable and secure businesses are, in reality, *marketing* businesses. This makes many professionals uncomfortable, and many have negative ideas and biases about it. Bad attitudes about marketing, lack of interest in it, resistance, avoidance are very severe handicaps; you might as well be a one-armed or even armless dentist. Your "relationship" with marketing – internal and external – is determinate of your income: below par, par, or way above par.

Fourth, it is critical *not* to confuse one's deliverables exchanged for money with the actual business one is in. Clarity of thought about this is vital. In your case, dentistry is only the deliverable – it is *not* the business. The business is really about the second and third items I just described. For this reason, no particular business is fundamentally different from any other.

Fifth, finally, the majority is always "wrong" – when it comes to money and to autonomy. That's why, with all the knowledge and technology advancements of the last 60 years, the financial facts of the general population and of every professional or occupational population within it stay unchanged: basically, 1% rich and independent, 4% earning a high income but often sacrificing too much for it, 15% earning a good living; 40% just getting by, and chronically frustrated and disappointed; and 40% essentially, chronically broke. Thus, 95% to 99% are "wrong". Trying to do things the way they are *supposed to be* done or the way they've *always been* done or the way a majority of peers do them but incrementally better or at a faster, harder-working pace has no liberating power whatsoever. Further, accepting frustrating, disappointing, imprisoning situations and excusing them as "well, just the nature of this beast" is bluntly stupid and shameful. Whatever you accept, you get more of. You need *not* accept anything less or different from what you want. The "authorities" who tell you that you must are themselves getting by, and chronically frustrated and disappointed, and misery loves company, or are charlatans peddling old wine with new labels because that's easier than breaking new ground and persuading people of entirely different trails. BEWARE!

So, this book by Dr. Biasucci gives you an overview, introduction and insider's look at the direct application of these five Great Truths to the dental practice. To a very different kind of dental practice.

Don't settle.

There is a fun mail-order catalog called "Things You Never Knew Existed." In many ways, this book is a catalog of "Possibilities You Never Knew Or Believed Existed" in dental practice. Go thorough it carefully, and as Dr. Seuss advised, see what you can see!

DAN S. KENNEDY

Dan S. Kennedy is a trusted strategic advisor to hundreds of 7-figure income professionals, entrepreneurs and CEO's. He is also the author of more than 20 books, including the No B.S. Guide to Ruthless Management of People and Profits (2nd Edition). Information at: NoBSBooks.com and GKIC.com.

SECTION 1

YOUR PERSONAL PRISON

CHAPTER 1

THE SOLO PRACTICE TRAP

HIGH HOPES

Do you remember the day you were accepted into dental school? The excitement of getting the acceptance letter in the mail and the feeling of being welcomed into a respected and esteemed profession is something I will never forget. That soaring feeling, however, wears off quite quickly in the real world, doesn't it?

The high hopes many dentists initially carry into the profession are often met with disillusionment. Most of us are secretly struggling. The lifestyle is what we all want: time with our families and a great income. It's essentially the best of both worlds, but what does it take to actually achieve these goals?

Income in the dental profession is inextricably linked to manual labour. We have to work longer and longer to reach our financial goals, which, in turn, erodes our lifestyles. This results in a never-ending treadmill of time and effort required to produce *every* dollar – *if you want more, you have to work more.*

It's A Trap Most Of Us Never Escape!

If you really want to carve out more time for your personal life, you will have to work less, and accept that your income will suffer. Dentists are often surprised to find after years in practice that they don't have the ability to take time off. They can't take their family on vacations *when they want*. They don't have the income to drive the car they want, live in the home they want, or buy the vacation home they want—let alone to *retire* when they want. As you know, many dentists are working into their late 60s and 70s, out of *financial necessity*! This is a truly sad trend.

YOU ARE YOUR BUSINESS

In this profession, your business *is YOU, the dentist*! It all rises and falls with YOU. You never get to have a bad day. Your income is determined by how many patients you treat. But don't forget: to run your business, you actually must perform what would be:

3 Full Time Jobs In Any Other Business!

You must play three strikingly different roles: the dentist working on patients, the business owner, and the business manager. Each role is critical to your success, but *you've actually only been prepared for one of them!*

Have you ever considered exactly how many hours you spend wearing these three hats? Most dentists spend 35-40 hours chair-side every week. They then spend an hour at the end of the day, as well as Friday—or part of their weekends—managing their practice's business needs. Add it all up. You are probably working 45-50 hours per week BEFORE you actually start working on improving your business!

Let me ask you a question: what will improve in your business, if you do not work on it?

In fact, studies of job satisfaction show dentists rank themselves lowest in areas of personal time and administrative responsibilities.[7] Are you one of them?

WHERE'S YOUR SAFETY NET?

And for all of your blood, sweat, and tears, you have...

No Safety Net For You And Your Family.

What happens if you get sick, need time off to spend with your family, want to take a vacation, or just slow down?

According to *solopreneur*, the average business owner takes less than 10 days of vacation per year.[14] Most employees in 'average jobs,' on the other hand, get 4-6 weeks off each year, *with benefits*. Many receive pensions as well.

Furthermore, the majority of business owners' operations can keep running when they are away. For dentists, however, <u>the business grinds to a halt when you are not there</u>. There is no income when you are not working, which leads to guilt about taking vacations, as well as emotional stress about not being available for your family.

And let's not forget, there is also

no security for your family if you become injured or disabled...

According to the US Social Security Administration, 1 in 4 of today's twenty-year-olds will become disabled before they retire.[15] This alarming statistic aptly conveys the need for every profession to have appropriate safety nets in place; yet most dentists go without.

PHYSICAL AND EMOTIONAL TOLLS OF THE PROFESSION

The profession is also physically demanding. You will spend years hunched over your patients. Even the best posture makes a 25-year career in a chair difficult at best. This situation is hard to avoid, because when you are not sitting and working on a patient, you are not earning. And yet, regardless of whether you're earning or not, you're still paying the overhead.

The practice of dentistry is emotionally draining over time as well. You've probably heard the common complaint, 'I hate the dentist,' almost every day. You're also probably familiar with the classic patients who behave as if everything that's happening in their mouth is your fault. Others may demand to be 'fixed' with the snap of a finger—as if you had a magic wand that could make all of their dental problems disappear with a slight wave.

We must also deal with complaints about the fees. Many patients are difficult or impossible to collect fees from, and these same patients are generally immediately unhappy if your schedule isn't running perfectly on time. It never ceases to amaze me that people will complain about a $200 filling not lasting a lifetime, but they fully expect to spend upwards of $600 to replace their smartphone every few years.

These unavoidable scenarios ultimately lead to emotional stress and fatigue. In fact, a recent study reported on in the *LA Times* cited the prevalence of depression among doctors to be at 29%![23] This is no way to live or work.

OTHER STRESSES

For most dentists, dealing with employees is one of the biggest sources of stress and frustration. According to a Gallup poll, 87% of employees are disengaged while on the job.[24] This has serious consequences. In fact, that level of disengagement results in an estimated 1/3 of your payroll dollars going to the wind – time wasted on idle chat, surfing the Internet, bumbling around, or just looking busy. It is also reported that 75% of employees will steal from you.[25]

As if that weren't enough, at any time you can be dragged into a lawsuit, which can take you away from your practice unexpectedly. And for the price of a stamp, any patient can thrust you into a year-long investigation with your dental board over *anything*, frivolous or not (you then get to pay a lawyer to prove your innocence).

When all of this is added together, it's clear that the STRESS in our profession is high. "Dentists are under extreme amounts of stress from working long hours, complaints from patients, and debt. Researchers have suggested that: stress, physical and emotional demands, patient complaints, perfectionism, debt, ease of access to various drugs, and higher rates of mental illness due to stress are all factors that attribute to a higher suicide rate among dentists." [13]

Now, I want you to ask yourself a question: what would your life look like without all of this stress? *How would it feel?* Keep on reading...

CHAPTER 2

THE SOLO PRACTICE MODEL IS DEAD

My friends,

This Is A Critical Time In Dentistry, And Not A Time For Complacency...

The Trends You CANNOT AFFORD TO IGNORE:

» **According to the ADA, 96% of dentists cannot afford to retire at age 65 and maintain their desired lifestyle!**

» **Corporate clinics** are competing on price, and furthering the commoditization of dentistry. They're also asking dentists to accept lower and lower incomes, and to become mere employees, resulting in a loss of their autonomy.

» **Insurance companies** are dictating lower and lower fees. There's an increasing number of adults uninsured, and an increased utilization of publicly funded plans as well, resulting in serious downward pressure on fees.

» There is a general **decrease in the utilization of dental care**. The percentage of adults who visit a dentist has been dropping for the past decade among all income groups. According to the Ontario Dental Association, many insured adults do not visit a dentist at all.

» There is a growing pressure across North America to expand the roles of **mid-level providers**, especially in the US.

» Gen X'ers (born 1965-1980) and Millennials (born 1981-2000) will have **reduced dental needs,** and are more likely to seek lower costs of care.

» Children born 2000 and later will have even less dental disease and demand for dental treatment as they age.

» Younger populations are more apt to prefer high-tech interactions, where they can **price shop through social media.**

» **The number of foreign-trained dentists continues to flood the market.**

» **There has been almost ZERO increase in the fees for dentists over the past 2 years.**

These may not be trends you can control. However, you must focus on the aspects of the profession you CAN control, if you want to combat them—primarily, how you can run your business better. This is what will ultimately determine what impact these trends have on your business.

REVERSE THE TREND

What Does This Mean To You?

No Increase In Fees, Combined With Constantly Rising Expenses, Will Continue Eroding Dentist's Incomes, More And More Every Year!

*You Are Working Harder And Harder To Give More Each Year To
Your Staff And Dental Supplier, And[1] Having Less And Less Time
For You And Your Family!*

I personally find this trend to be appalling and insulting to the profession. We have all worked far too hard to end up in this trap of trading our time and effort for every dollar we earn.

If You Want To Reverse This Trend And Get Out Of The Time And Effort Trap, You Need To Think AND *DO* Differently!

According to Einstein, The Definition Of Insanity Is Doing The Same Thing Over And Over, And Expecting A Different Or Better Result...

If you want next year to be better, something significant in your practice has to change! But what do you change, in order to grow your business and solve these problems? *It is NOT your clinical skills...*

Consider This:

According to the Harvard Business Review, every business, including a dental practice, will lose 50% of their patient base every 5 years![2,11] Just staying neutral requires constant work – if your practice *is not growing*, it *is* getting smaller!

If 50% of your practice will leave every 5 years, and we average that to 10% per year, then you must be growing by at least 10%, just to stay on an even keel.

BUT:

At the same time, your family and business expenses are also increasing...

The cost of living goes up by 2-3% each year.

The cost of doing business (supplies, lab and staff) also increases by an average of 3%.

That may not seem like a lot, but if you now factor in fee erosion or no increase in fees, which is very common—it's actually more like 20%, JUST TO STAY LEVEL!

That is, just to take home what you did last year.

Do You Have a Strategy?

What is your strategy for increasing by 20% over the next year?

Even if you have a strategy, do you realize you're only going to be bringing in the same salary as last year? Would you like a raise, perhaps?

When you consider this reality, you really have only two options:

Option 1: You can work harder and harder every year, at the expense of your family and your health (and sanity). That doesn't sound like much fun to me.

Option 2: You can start running your practice like a business, and FINALLY break the link between the earning of every dollar to holding a handpiece. You can start creating a business that *supports your lifestyle*, not one that *consumes it*.

CHAPTER 3

WHO AM I, AND WHY SHOULD YOU CARE?

MY JOURNEY TO A 7-FIGURE NET INCOME (WITHOUT PRACTICING DENTISTRY)

First off, as I said earlier, I am a dentist, like you.

Let me give you a bit of my backstory...

Dentistry was never really on my mind, until I had the experience of getting braces, and teeth removed for braces. Over those four years of treatment, I found myself in and out of dental offices and dental specialty offices, for what seemed like forever.

However, with each visit, I found myself completely in awe of the process that ushered me from a kid with ugly buck teeth and a retruded jaw to having a smile I could be proud of. I really looked up to these professionals, who made such a big difference in my life.

I also had a grand perception of my dentist's lifestyle, because it was very different from the construction background in which I grew up. In fact, I was so intrigued, I remember asking him what he thought about the profession, as I was interested in possibly making it a career choice. I asked him this at twelve years of age, and I'll never forget his answer. To my amazement, he told me dentistry was not as rewarding as he would have liked, and that he wouldn't have chosen it if he could do it again...

As a naive child, I didn't really appreciate the magnitude of that comment, and ultimately wouldn't, until I had become a practicing dentist some thirteen years later. So I decided to disregard his comment. I was bound and determined to become a dentist.

I applied to dental schools, and had really high hopes of staying in Ontario for my education. If at all possible, I wanted to stay at Western. I sent off my applications and got a few acceptance letters, and a few rejections. I got my rejection from Western on my birthday. I'll never forget that.

Consequently, I hoped and prayed. I don't know how, but I got accepted to Western one month later, and was off to become a dentist. It was the happiest moment in my education.

When I graduated, I wasn't wasting any time. I wanted to work hard, be as busy as possible, and make a name for myself. I wanted to own a practice, help people by being a great dentist, and make some real money. I had a very clear picture of the lifestyle I would have as a dentist—not having to work much beyond the hours that I wanted to keep, and having a lot of free time with a great income. In my mind, it seemed like all of my hard work in school would pay off for life.

After a few years, I found myself the owner of a business, with no understanding of what was actually required to run it. It was not pretty. I had to make up a huge gap in my knowledge of business in a short amount of time. As a result, I worked around the clock in the office and at home—until the early hours of the morning every day, in order to make the business as successful as I could. I did this for years, because I thought it was what I needed to do. The more I worked, the more I earned, and then I realized I was TRAPPED! For my income to go up, I had to treat more patients. Sure, I could add an associate—so I tried that, and it failed miserably, three times. I was working 40 hours a week on patients, and another 20-30 hours on trying to grow my practice. My personal life and my new marriage were paying the price. It was then that my health took a drastic turn for the worse.

After an especially stressful time in my career, my wife and I took a vacation, something we did every quarter to get away and decompress. This time would be different. We loved to scuba dive, and after having been on many dives in the preceding years, the first dive on this trip would be my last.

I suffered a severe decompression injury that landed me in the hospital for the week, instead of on the beach. I would return to Toronto for more hyperbaric treatments, and would then go on to spend the next six weeks in a hyperbaric chamber for two hours per day. The real icing on the cake came after investigating the cause of my injury. According to my dive computer, this was a textbook dive profile. It was something I had done many times. But I was told by two dive specialists that the only instances they've seen this kind of result from a normal dive is when an individual is "stressed out and running on empty." Although there is no definitive study on this, they had both witnessed this pattern in otherwise healthy young men.

The side effects were so pronounced at one point that I was told to consider another line of work. It took me one full year to recover.

As it turned out, the stress of my 'average' practice nearly killed me. Further down the road, I was diagnosed as celiac, and suffered from a few other autoimmune issues—all of which were primarily the result of chronic stress from that time in my life.

It was through that time that I did some real introspective thinking about what I wanted in my life. The stress I was living with (that I thought was just 'part of the job') was literally killing me. I was growing more isolated each day. The real kicker was that I had achieved many of the goals I set out to achieve—but I was aiming for an illusion.

I decided right then that things had to change, and fast. I made a commitment to myself, and my family, that I would fix this. I remember thinking, "If this is it, I have left so much on the table. I want to make my life count for something. I want to make a true impact on others, who find themselves in this place in their lives."

Over the course of 24 months, I took my practice from an 'average' solo practice to a multi-doctor, multi-specialty, self-managing organization, producing over 7 million dollars in a year. As I write this, are currently planning to add another six chairs to this location, for a total of twenty.

I am now enjoying the best health in which I have ever been. I have twice the free time to spend with my family, with more than twice the income. The best part: I experience no stress with my business, and **no longer have to practice a single day if I don't desire to do so**. Even if I stopped practicing, my income would still be TEN times the national average for a dentist.

I now only have to spend **one day per month running my business. This day is devoted to leading my greater team and my leadership team**. I take the entire summer off. I no longer trade hours of my life for an hourly wage—**this is the difference between having a job and owning a business.**

Since developing these systems, our new patient numbers went from about 40 per month to an average of 200 per month. More importantly, we maintain a 50% referral percentage.

Our patient retention is up 100%, and we have doubled our hygiene department to meet demand.

We have a steady stream of associate doctors *APPLYING* to work in our office, so I get the pick of the litter. We also have no difficulty attracting specialists to work for us. Each month we have an average of 65 people applying to work with us.

This is not by accident—it is by *strategic design.*

Our marketing strategy has turned my practice into the trusted authority in the area—all without having to compromise myself professionally.

All of this has been achieved in a small town of 75,000, **with 40 other dentists and a lousy economy, where our second largest employer went belly-up. In fact, our largest employer is in bankruptcy**

protection as I write this. Practices around us are struggling, and we are having our best years ever. The 2,000+ patients joining our office every year is literally 2.6% of the population, joining my practice *EVERY YEAR*.

You see, **I spent every hour that I was off sick studying marketing and business building.** Since then, I have read over 100 business books, spent hundreds of hours with coaches, and studied many leading businesses, absorbing everything I could apply into my business. The total result of about 1,000 hours and over one million dollars spent is the "*Elite Practice*". It represents the distilled knowledge of all of my studying, implementation, testing, and successes.

I completely restructured my business, and put it back together multiple times. I have made mistakes. **At one time I had 21 people quit from my office in a 6-month period!** I was devastated. To make matters worse, it happened during a time when we were getting quarterly one-day trainings from a consultant, **so not only were these one-day blitzes not fixing anything, they were all going to waste**.

What I came to learn, after becoming a true student of leadership, systems, and processes, is that this mistake was a direct result of my **lack of clear, tested, and proven systems** for hiring and training team members, and building a culture of excellence.

Today we have a team of thirty-five, and all members are all completely engaged in our vision. Our business culture now joins the high ranks of companies like Google and Apple.

I talk with so many colleagues who, like the dentist from my past, hate what they are doing. They regret getting involved in this profession. This deeply saddens me.

It's easy to see why they regret choosing dentistry. When you graduate from dental school, you must become a clinical treatment provider, manager, HR person, marketing person, and so forth. These are full-time jobs in and of themselves. The stress that comes with carrying such a workload is significant.

It's no wonder the quality of life is below adequate for so many dentists.

However, I am proof that there is another way...

I don't want anyone to get the impression that I am unique in any way. I know there are more skilled and intelligent dentists out there. I have achieved a level of success that is unique, because I was pushed to the point of breaking. This experience made me tear apart every aspect of my business in order to figure out what works and what doesn't. I now know that no one should settle for anything less than the life they want.

My greatest ability is to study what is working well in other businesses and industries, and apply that to my business.

I have invested the time and money to distill all of the knowledge I've consumed—down to the most profitable business skillset, systems, and processes that will empower you to realize your dream lifestyle and practice. These systems give you the freedom to have a fulfilling lifestyle, rather than having to live a life orchestrated around your practice.

WILL YOU HAVE THE TIME, RESOURCES, AND STAMINA TO FIGURE IT OUT ON YOUR OWN?

I can tell you that this journey, at times, felt overwhelming for me. I did consider giving up, selling the practice, and moving on. But I am too stubborn for that, so I pushed through.

Napoleon Hill said it best: "Most people achieve their greatest success just one step beyond their greatest failure." This is the absolute truth, and my experience proves it.

Based on my journey, and the short time in which I achieved these results, I know with absolute certainty that anyone can have the practice they want, by applying the right, proven systems. These systems will work in any market, in any town.

It is my passion and purpose now to see as many dentists as possible break free of the solo practice trap. In the chapters that follow, I'll reveal how you can do just that.

CHAPTER 4

FIGHT BACK AND GAIN CONTROL

DENTISTRY IS A BUSINESS

The first step toward shifting your experience of success, is recognizing that dentistry is a business like any other. Running a successful dental practice is NOT just about the dentistry!

Trouble is inevitable when dentists spend an average of eight years in school, learning everything *but* business skills. In fact, most dental students will spend 1/50th of their time talking about practice management, with the majority of that discussion focused on the legislation governing the profession, basic human rights, and labour laws.[13]

There is virtually no talk of leadership, hiring, training, team development, business growth, systematizing, maximizing profits, or marketing – all of which are equally as important to the success of your practice as your clinical ability. If you aren't looking at these critical areas in your practice consistently—then who is?

Most dentists are doing the dentistry, yet failing to address crucial business areas of their practices. They're not focusing on the profit centers, team engagement, or the degree to which systems are being created and followed. Many aren't even learning how to market and promote their services, so that they can *actually be dentists*.

Dentists also don't have the same amount of time available to devote toward the management of their practice, compared with a professional, who opens a real estate office or insurance agency. These professionals can hire representatives to actually sell homes or insurance policies while they work *ON* their businesses. Dentists, on the other hand, have their hands full performing dentistry.

The End Result: New And Woefully Unequipped Staff Members Are Making Decisions That Impact Your Bottom Line!

Decisions, such as what to say on the phone and how to handle your number one asset, your patients, cannot be left to chance! Most dentists place the success of their businesses in the hands of $18/hr employees, who have no skin in the game. These employees have no understanding of how they impact the bottom line, and many really don't care, because they're only concerned about what's in it for them.

ARE YOU INVESTING IN TOOLS FOR YOUR SUCCESS?

Think about how you felt during your first day on the job. How confident were you? You knew what to do, but you also knew you were green. Maybe you're like me. Even after *thousands* of hours of clinical training, you still take more than the mandated minimum amount of CE hours to stay updated every year—because we all want to excel at what we do.

Now compare that to the miniscule amount of business education we had in school. And more importantly – how much business CE have you taken since you graduated?

How Big Is The Gap?

Bottom line: if you want to change your business, then you must invest in <u>your business skill set!</u>

This means spending time and money learning about tools and strategies that enable you to work smarter, not harder—tools that allow your business to start working *for* you, instead of the other way around.

A CHANGE OF PERSPECTIVE

How would you rate your business skillset compared to your clinical skills?

In order to combat the myriad of issues we just addressed, your business skills must be *better than* your clinical skills. It is your business skillset that brings people into your office, so you can practice dentistry!

You must invest significant time and energy into developing your business skillset, in order close the gap, and to continually *maintain your edge*.

TIMES HAVE CHANGED

A strong business practice was not as important in years gone by, when there was less competition, and a nonexistence of the large corporate practices that are now popping up like weeds. Now dentists are like pharmacies; there's one on every corner. The pharmacy owner must know how to attract customers, how to maximize profit margins, and how to keep customers loyal. The same is true for dentists.

These skills are no longer optional. You can excel at running your business, or you can work for someone else—these are your only options.

Chapter 5

The 4 Foundations of The Elite Practice

What Is The Elite Practice?

I have often been asked: "What exactly is Elite Practice?". It's a fair question. It is not simply a random creation. Here is the continuum I like to reference with respect to the evolution of a practice:

Solo >> Solo+Associates >> Super GP >> Elite

I look at it in terms of market share commanded by these models, and more importantly by the stability and resilience of each model in the marketplace.

The Solo Practice model is the one that we are all most familiar with, and the typical, traditional model of practice. This is one dentist, with a handful of staff members, working 'banker's hours' that revolve around the dentist owner's choices. This model is dying and based on market trends, will continue to be consolidated at a rapid pace over the next decade.

The addition of associates to the solo practice model adds the ability to cover the hours that the market wants, and to increase capacity beyond the owner's own personal production.

In the "Super GP" model is the evolution of the Solo Practice, though associates, to bring all services under one roof and essentially offer all services that a patient might need. The stability in the market is much greater because the business is designed around market preferences, there is greater degree of systemization, there is usually a leadership structure, and the revenue/profit generated can be much greater than the other models.

Building further on the "Super GP" model is what I call the "Elite Practice". The differences are another order of magnitude greater than the previous model. Elite practices are systems-driven and market-driven. There is strong leadership and team culture. The business focuses on developing and growing human assets. Processes are very intentional and clearly defined. Capacity is maximized and all services are offered in-house through a variety of associates and associate-specialists.

This model can serve both the lower-income population on government dental plans, as well as the higher-end, higher-revenue procedures with authority-based direct marketing. The middle ground 'average patient' is also very well served.

The revenue/profit possible in this model in virtually unlimited. While that might be very attractive, equally important in my opinion is the stability this model offers in the marketplace. Because both ends of the spectrum are catered to, individually and uniquely, but under one brand, it is far less likely that price competition will be an issue. It is also less likely that the top 5% of consumers will not choose this type of practice. The middle ground is covered by an excellent, market-driven and service-driven practice. This type of model is best capable to weather economic downturns, heavier competition, corporate consolidation, and even disruptive changes that have not yet been considered.

This model is the most resistant to everything that is coming and will come to disrupt our profession. It also allows for the most autonomy and financial freedom. As a result, if you wanted to sell this type of practice, the value would be much, much greater.

WHERE ARE YOU? WHERE DO YOU WANT TO BE?

Take a moment to imagine how your life would look, if you could excel at running your business. You would be enjoying a 7-figure income. You would have the flexibility to take vacations or time off when you desired. You would also have ample time to devote to your family and important relationships, as well as other meaningful life areas.

So why aren't you there yet?

First off, every dentist I know works really hard. Why, then, is there a huge income gap in the profession? Why is the average income only $150,000 per year, yet some dentists take home ten times that? Why are some dentists enjoying great success, while others struggle to keep afloat?

There is a distinct pattern shared between dentists with a 7-figure net income, and a contrasting pattern shared by those who make a fraction of that. We will address these patterns shortly, so stay tuned.

THE SUCCESS FORMULA

We all spent years honing our craft and taking all of the latest and greatest CE curriculums. We received AGD Fellowships (I have one of those too), but at the end of the day, we've realized (hopefully!) that these tools don't amplify our successes—we're still striving for greater freedom and income.

Now, I believe it is important to be credentialed and to be an excellent clinician, but this is only half of the success equation. We all know the dentist who isn't the greatest clinician, but his practice is busy. Why is that?

The other half of the dentistry success formula is your business skillset. √

The inability to properly identify and evaluate key business areas needing improvement in your practice is like a fog on your path to freedom. A clear understanding of the skills necessary to strategically grow your business is the first step toward freedom.

The biggest and best-run practices are heavily focused on growing business knowledge, as well as incorporating the best systems and practices to *fast-track their way to success, rather than re-invent the wheel.*

The dentists who embrace this change will be the ones who thrive.

IT IS NOT ENOUGH TO BE THE BEST DENTIST

The most successful dentists – the ones enjoying the highest income and quality of life—are the dentists who have the best business skills.

An essential step toward building a robust practice is to start closing the gap between your clinical and business skills. There will very likely be a huge gap if your last 'business' education came from dental school, trade journals, or a 'practice management' seminar.

To move your practice into a true business, you must focus on the 4 foundations of an Elite Practice:

1. **Systems**
2. **Training**
3. **Leadership**
4. **Marketing**

 ← 4 pillars

SECTION 2

SYSTEMS

CHAPTER 6

THERE'S A SYSTEM FOR THAT

THE KRYPTONITE OF YOUR PRACTICE

At the foundations of every strong business are solid systems. Let's look at the McDonald's example. This is a business that was built on minimum-wage teenagers following a paint-by-numbers system that allows the very same hamburger to be produced in Dallas or in Rome. Absolutely nothing is left to chance or to the discretion of the employee. If you don't follow the system, you deliver an inconsistent experience, and therefore, you fail to deliver the correct product.

Inconsistency results in declining business. For the exact same reasons, every single process in your office should have a system—right down to who fills the refreshment bar for patients, along with when and how it is done.

PUTTING YOURSELF IN YOUR PATIENT'S SHOES

As customers, we've all experienced going out to dinner, having a great meal, and then waiting forever for the check. It is annoying, especially if you want to get home and relieve the babysitter, or you're tired and have to get up early the next day. It's also what you remember most – not the great food or the conversation; but the waiting.

The place I go to for lunch—and have for years—is close to my office, and they have you in and out in 30 minutes, always. That's what you want to deliver to your patients: an experience that is no-fail.

Why is this so important? First of all, it increases your refer-ability. When people refer you, they are vouching for you, and putting their reputation on the line. If the person they refer has a great experience with you, they look good. If it is a bad experience, then it's an awkward situation.

Being consistent is critical. Here's the key to achieving it: you accomplish consistency by establishing processes that run your practice, not people.

ESTABLISHING YOUR SYSTEM

You can create every single system yourself, or you can borrow what is already proven from someone who is willing to share. The systems and training platform that we use in my own practice can be found at www.ElitePracticeFormulaBook.com.

To create consistent experiences, we must not depend on specific people who are highly skilled in an area. Instead, we must establish processes that govern the delivery of service, and then have competent people run the processes. This frees you from needing to have a team of superstars. It also saves you from the havoc of turnover. It is far better to have a 'good' team working excellent processes than a superstar team doing it their way. Consistency and intention will ALWAYS win.

Another upside of having strong systems is you don't have to deal with diva attitudes in the workplace. If you have ever had a team of superstars, you know how difficult it is to manage strong personalities. Robust systems allow you to offer minimal feedback without affecting egos. It is far more conducive to your sanity to have a systems-based business with good people possessing great attitudes, all working within that system.

How do you find great attitudes and hard workers? There's a system for that too...

Your Current Hiring Process

Think about your current process for hiring right now. Do you put a job ad in the paper or on the Internet job boards? Do you weed through stacks of resumes, conduct interview after interview, and then make your decision, solely based on the "performances" you saw?

How many hours have you spent (WASTED) interviewing candidates that looked good on a resume, and turned out to be a total disaster in the interview? How many made it past the interview, only to crash in the first month?

Your Team

Consider the many years you have employed people. Do you view your staff as a necessary evil, or your greatest asset?

Would your life be different if the caliber of your team were at a level at which they could not only run, but GROW your business? How would it feel to have your employees grow your business under your leadership, without you having to manage every detail, or do all of the "heavy lifting"?

What if you had the freedom to go away on a vacation, or attend your daughter's dance recital, without having to pull out your smartphone to put out a fire at the office?

How much are your current employees STEALING from you with their negativity and lack of buy-in? How about the drama and gossip? This is the cancer that destroys a team, but get it rooted out, and your team will SOAR to new heights. Systems enable you to do so.

Customer Service is Everything

Your business is only as good as the people serving your customer.

Sure, you can just focus on attracting more clients, and change nothing else. You can spend more and more on marketing to get more people through your doors, but you will lack the incentive to make them want to come back, let alone refer their family and friends.

Or you can empower your team to provide truly legendary service that builds **loyalty and refer-ability.** You can also target bigger and more affluent clients that will pay larger fees. It has been shown, time and time again, that people invest greater money and loyalty in _experiences_, not products.

Just look at Disney – the prime example of hiring the best people to create exceptional service and experience – *WITHIN THEIR SYSTEMS*. They have an intensely loyal following with comparatively little spent on marketing.

BUILDING THE ELITE PRACTICE TEAM

If you want to have the best team and bring in top revenue, your hiring process must focus on four areas:

1) Attracting applicants.

2) Systematically narrowing them down to the top-tier candidates.

3) Following a step-by-step process and employing proven psychological tactics to select the best one or two candidates.

4) Determining if the candidate will be a true fit for your team through utilizing a statistically valid and legal employee role comparison method.

5) Offering employment and conducting the onboarding process.

This is not an easy process, but the investment in time and money will far outweigh the cost of a bad hire. If you would like to know the detailed process I use in my own practice, visit www.ElitePracticeFormulaBook.com.

The key—regardless of whether you want to build a big business or a busy but highly functioning small practice—is following the McDonald's example: employ strong systems that run your business, and have good enough people operating them. I hesitate to say 'good enough,' because when you find great people, you can move mountains. I do want to stress the point, though, that the **systems** should be running the business—not an employee's superstar ability. If your system involves a superstar employee handling a sector of your practice, what will you do when he or she leaves?

Great training systems insulate you from the chaos of turnovers. The more automated your training system is, the better. I started this chapter with the heading "The Kryptonite of Your Practice." By now I hope you see that I was referring to a lack of systems. Refusing to have systems run your business will do more than make your office run poorly. It can be truly toxic to life and success of your practice. It's like kryptonite to Superman, sapping the health and strength right out of it.

CHAPTER 7

A FAIRY TALE EXPERIENCE

CREATING A WORLD CLASS EXPERIENCE

There is no question that the experience patients have with your practice – with you and your team – absolutely determines your success. You want people coming out of your practice saying, "That's the best dental experience I've ever had."

If you want to nail this to perfection, you must have a clear vision of what you want to achieve. You must know what, exactly, you want your patients to experience.

Put yourself in your patient's shoes, and envision the experience that your patients will have as they get out of their car, enter your building, open your door, walk inside, are greeted by your team, move to your lounge, and so on. See it like a movie playing out in your mind. Record the movie on paper. Turn this into the operating manual for your team.

Shortly, we're going to walk through an entire process of mapping out your patient experience. This will not only enable you to always deliver the perfect experience to your patients, but will result in many referrals. Your patients will be so excited about their time spent in your practice that they'll want to offer this experience to their friends and contacts. Your patient experience then becomes your referral machine.

THE THREE PATIENT EXPERIENCES

When you are presenting a world-class experience, *you are actually selling a feeling, not fillings.* You want to make your patients feel markedly better about themselves after having spent time in your practice. This creates intense loyalty that affords price elasticity. It is also kryptonite to corporate dentistry.

With this in mind, let's talk about the three feelings a trip to your practice can evoke. After every patient interaction, your patient will leave your practice feeling unhappy, neutral (AKA "satisfied"), or happy. The number one goal must always be to have EVERY patient leave your office in the happy category.

You do not want patients leaving unhappy. First of all, if they're unhappy, they're not going to do business with you again. They'll also tell other people about their unsatisfactory experience. The worst part: they will kill your future growth, because you are certainly not going to get referrals from these people.

The second experience, which generally occurs in most practices, is a patient feeling satisfied with your service. You don't want satisfied either. Yes, they will show up, and pay you money. They may even come back and do business with you again—IF they're not swayed by another dentist's marketing, or their brother-in-law's referral to his dentist. These patients see you as 'any other dentist,' which doesn't breed loyalty. Satisfied patients won't go out of their way to tell other people about you either.

When you wow your patients, though, they leave with *smiles on their faces*. They get more than they anticipated. This is when your business really picks up.

CREATING YOUR 'PATIENT EXPERIENCE BLUEPRINT'

The only way you can achieve this level of satisfaction is by making your patient's experience a priority.

Start your patient experience design by asking yourself, along with your team, two simple questions:

1. What does everyone LOVE about going to the dentist/our office?
2. What does everyone HATE about going to the dentist?

I understand the answer to the first question might be laughable at first read – nobody loves going to the dentist. But on serious reflection, if you can list at least five reasons people love coming to your office, you are well on your way to realizing a major area of potential in your business. Simple things, like "The doctor and his assistant always make me laugh," or "They always greet me by my name," are not trivial. They are the touch-points that create relationships and lead to a 'wow' experience.

Take this exercise to the next level by imagining what your patients would REALLY love, if they thought it was possible. This is your opportunity to imagine a 'dream experience' for your patients. Don't limit your thinking by saying, "Well, I can't do that," or "That's impossible." Just put everything that comes to mind on the table, and then ask yourself, "If I could do it...how would I do it?"

You have three options whenever you have a patient in your practice. Are you going to give them less than what they expected, exactly what they expected, or more than what they expected?

If you want to nurture lifetime relationships and generate practice-shifting referrals, you must deliver world-class service at every touch-point.

This can be achieved through carefully engineering every single step of your process and leaving nothing to chance. For example, in my own practice, the New Patient Experience System is a step-by-step blueprint, spanning 48 typed pages. There is a system and a script for everything. We do not hold our people to rigid scripts, but we do require a general consistency in conversation.

This entire system is detailed in a step-by-step manner. Learn more at www.ElitePracticeFormulaBook.com.

CHAPTER 8

SYSTEMATIC PRACTICE GROWTH

While patient retention rates are poor in every average-performing business, they don't have to be in your practice. Studies show that 96% of unhappy customers don't complain, and that 91% of unhappy customers simply don't come back. Price is not the main reason for customer defection; it is actually poor quality of service. Furthermore, a full 55% of customers would pay more to guarantee a better service.[16]

The fact that your patients will travel for your dental work may have less to do with clinical skillsets than you think—and a lot more to do with **the experience they have with your business**. After all, they can't judge your clinical excellence.

With this knowledge, it must be an absolute priority to improve every aspect of how your patients interact with your practice, including:

» How skilfully your phones are answered (and verifying results)

» An intake process that sets the stage for each new patient to have maximum compliance with your treatment plan

» The first impression of your office

» Appearance and cleanliness

» Technology

» Highly systematized operations for a seamless and consistent experience across providers and team members

» Highly-trained team composed of high performers

» Patient feeling the appointment is about them and leaving your practice feeling great about the time they spent with you and your team

» Amenities and fine touches

» Follow up and care calls

» Anticipating the patient's needs

» Developing strong relationships

» No wait time

» Acknowledging and correcting any issues that arise immediately and appropriately

*The delivery of an excellently choreographed experience for every patient is the key to successfully reversing the trend toward commoditization of your business!

EVERY VISIT COUNTS

With a general decrease in the number of visits to private dental offices, **every visit to your practice must count**. Your team must be highly trained to help each patient identify and communicate his/her goal. Your team must also know how to facilitate case presentations by discussing options your practice offers to meet each goal. The more services you offer, the easier this is. Furthermore, the more skillful your team—including being highly trained in all procedures, along with the ability to deliver excellent patient experiences—the more they can build value for these options, and assist in successful case acceptance. **There is a science to case acceptance** that cannot be underestimated.

Corporate clinics, government clinics, and mid-level providers are all delivering services at the lowest possible fees, and doing so **makes it difficult to compete with you on the patient experience.** EXCEPT when the experience in your practice is similar to that in a corporate or government clinic—then you have taken out the areas of comparison that are to your advantage, and all that is left is price; *and you will lose in that game.*

Instead, get out of the price game altogether, and deliver an experience that not only retains patients, but encourages them to refer.

Consider this: customers that rate your business 5 out of 5 are SIX TIMES more likely to do business with you again and to remain loyal, compared with those who rate you only 4.8 out of 5.[16]

Delivering a superior patient experience requires a well-choreographed set of systems. Have you carefully engineered and clearly documented your process for

» Attracting patients,

» Converting prospective patients to active patients,

» How your team interacts with patients at every touch-point—from walking in the door to walking out as enthusiastic ambassadors of your practice, or

» Patient Retention?

FOCUS ON YOUR REVENUE

Systemization and patient experience are only part of the puzzle.

The best way to combat the increasing costs of running a practice is to increase revenue. This is not to say cost control isn't critical; however, the greatest impact you can make on your practice is **increasing revenue**. There is only so much to gain by cutting costs. You still need to pay for supplies, rent, staff, etc., and while you can trim fat, you certainly don't want to trim muscle.

Consider that a <u>2% increase in customer retention rate has the</u> <u>same effect as decreasing costs by 10%</u>, and you can see there are better places on which to focus your time and energy than simply cutting costs.[16]

THE REVENUE BLUEPRINT

Here are key areas that must be strategically addressed, in order to boost your revenue:

a. Leveraging Profit Generators with systems for hygiene recall, treatment plan follow-up, lost patient reactivation, etc.

b. Increasing billing per hour and the ability to offer same-day treatment with systems for speed and efficiency.

c. Increasing service mix to create a one-stop shop.

d. Maximizing the profit potential for each patient by systematically offering every service to every patient, as part of a proper new patient/existing patient appointment.

e. Having a system to ensure your patients know about all of the services you offer in your practice. Are they going to be the one patient who went to get veneers from a 'cosmetic dentist' and not you?

f. Monitoring key statistics daily to measure the performance of your business—*automatically.*

Another key strategic concept for revenue growth is to move out of the time and effort economy and into the results economy. That is, rather than trading your time for every dollar, leverage yourself through other people, to get results for which you are compensated. This is a strategy that can be applied to all aspects of your business and personal life.

In order to achieve this overall vision, a large chunk of the puzzle relies on your ability to lead your team and your business through proven systems. As your leadership skills improve, you will find that **the scaling**

up of your business becomes simple and strategic, as opposed to overwhelming. We'll address these concepts in greater depth in the chapters to come.

SECTION 3
TRAINING

CHAPTER 9

BUILDING THE ULTIMATE TEAM

Can a new hire walk onto your team and be useful on day one?

How would your practice change, if new hires could join your team and be onboard in less than a week, without having to follow Mary or Sally around until they 'got it'?

Believe it or not, all of this is possible. Before we delve into 'the how's,' though, let's address what doesn't work.

THE TRIBAL TRAINING METHOD

Most businesses train employees for a day or two, and then expect them to fully operate in their new positions. Take a moment to consider this. Do you think these employees are prepared to masterfully engage with their new responsibilities?

The industry-training norm in dental practices is the 'tribal' method: the new employee sits beside a present employee, from whom they are supposed to learn via observation. There is no actual structure in place that specifies what, exactly, needs to be learned, and in what order. There is often no clear vision, via a clearly detailed system, for a desired end result, either.

Typically, the 'trainer' learned through observation as well. At this point, the original system has become a distant, diluted version of the owner's original vision.

What kind of a result do you expect a scenario like this to produce?

Here's what all dentists need to realize: each person on their team that comes into contact with a patient directly impacts THEIR BOTTOM LINE; therefore, all team members need to operate within a strategic system that ensures outstanding work performances 100% of the time.

Are you satisfied with who is determining your profit, and the level of experience and engagement your patients are receiving?

If your answer is "No," or even "Maybe," it's time to seek out a new approach. The ultimate training method is a step-by-step, automated process that is virtually hands-off for existing staff. By the end of this training, new employees would know the exact system you expect to be followed, which enables them to be far more valuable at the onset of their hiring. This automated method would require a minimal investment of time by existing staff to train new hires, further reducing stress on the existing staff when new hires are brought on.

WHAT MOST PRACTICES ARE MISSING

Many businesses simply do not make the commitment to training—not only new staff, but also re-training their existing staff. This is at their own peril.

If fact, most practices have little or no ongoing staff training. If there is any, it is inconsistent at best.

Here's the hard truth: the only way to improve your business is to make a commitment to training. Consider that the average small business employee gets 27 hours of training each year. [21] The top businesses invest double that or more, and in return, they enjoy less turnover, and increased bottom line results.

THE SECRET TO HIGH IMPACT ORGANIZATIONS

Learning and employee development are at the core of high impact organizations' efficacy.

For example, **the Cheesecake Factory invests an average of $2000/ employee annually on training. As a result, the chain enjoys sales of $1000 per square foot, almost double the restaurant industry average.**

It is among the 100 Best Companies to Work For. They devote, on average, 73 hours/salaried workers, and 58 hours/hourly workers, on training and development each year, respectively. [17]

Why do the Cheesecake Factory, and other highly successful companies, heavily invest in training? Employee development leads to higher customer satisfaction, more innovation, lower costs, and faster growth.

It's also the gateway to sales and product knowledge, which lead to increased revenues and market share.

Equally important, service training results in exceptional customer experiences, which lead to brand loyalty.

Leadership training can also help employees grow more qualified for internal promotions, reducing turnover by as much as 65%. [17] **(The cost of a bad hire is as much as 50% of their annual salary, even if they are only present for a short time. [18])**

Now that you have some examples of companies that have built thriving businesses based on the experiences they offer to their customers, ask yourself:

How many hours are you investing in your team?

How effective has this training been?

How much profit are you leaving on the table as a result?

Bottom line: if you want consistent, top-notch performance, you must have consistent, strategic, and ongoing training!

WEEKEND TRAININGS AREN'T ENOUGH

Now, consider this – **at the Ritz Carlton, one of the world's best examples of service excellence, an employee gets 120 hours of formal training _each year_, and the training is ongoing, indefinitely.** [22]

In our profession, the most common methods of formal training are hiring a consultant or attending a seminar. If you take the consultant route, he or she will send someone to your practice for a "training day": a one-day blitz from which you will achieve a little bump in energy from your team, only to find it wear off after the first weekend passes.

The seminar approach is equally frustrating. You've probably sat through several seminars or one-day trainings. Perhaps you even closed your office for a day to attend one. Now let me ask you: how much have you _actually_ implemented from these trainings?

I'm sure most of the content was good, but can you say you actually implemented more than 20% of the training? The problem with these methods is that they use a 'one-and-done' approach, while the brain needs multiple exposures to new instruction in order to create a new habit.

If you're familiar with Malcolm Gladwell's 10,000-hour theory – it takes 10,000 hours of practice to become an expert at something—then, at the very least, you realize one single exposure to new techniques or information is not going to teach your team anything.

You, as the doctor and business owner, will probably learn more, because you are paying for the training. There is more on the line for you. Your team, on the other hand, will ultimately learn little from a one-off training.

The Hard Truth: most attendees of a weekend seminar or training day in the office implement only about 10% of what they learn. This is mainly due to the lack of accountability built into the training. There is no structure for the implementation, and no support built around getting results.

Instead there is just a sense of being overwhelmed.

Have you ever had this experience?

I know I have spent hundreds of thousands of dollars on seminars and 'training days,' only to receive minuscule returns.

THE SOLUTION: THE AUTOMATIC TRAINING SYSTEM

Get the most out of your training investment through a sequenced and steady stream of small instruction bites. This allows for regular, targeted instruction to be delivered through a system that marries learning and implementation with accountability. During each step of the process, the results are always measured, which ensures training success before moving on to the next step.

The training process, which is of equal importance, must also be repeated, for maximum efficacy. Even with accountability, **employees will never retain 100% of what they are taught during the first exposure**. According to *Brain World Magazine*, multiple exposures to the same information, as well as reinforcement, are necessary to form the neural connections that equate to memory. This is why listening to a seminar is of little benefit. Value enters the picture when learners take pen to paper[20] and are given the opportunity to role-play, while being monitored on their results *over time*.

When training your team to offer a new service, or when rolling out new protocols in your practice, every process must have a clearly-written end result that is achieved when the process is completed correctly. This result is a clear, definitive end point, which everyone works toward. Everyone who runs that specific process must be trained according to this standard.

All of these systemized approaches to training make it extremely easy to achieve accountability, and to correct any issues with your team. This is exactly why I created the Elite Practice Academy digital learning platform. This platform offers built-in accountability through quizzes and exams, which lead to certifications. It also incorporates repetition into its learning model, by requiring recertification at least bi-annually.

With the Elite Practice Academy Digital Learning Platform, you are insulated against turnover, because from the day a new team member starts, they are easily added to the system, and instantly begin their training. Within a few days, you have a very capable team member who knows the system and clearly understands what is expected of them. You are also confident that they have been exposed to all of the material in the platform and have been *tested on it.*

How does this compare to your current onboarding process? Have you ever considered the effect turnover has on your training budget? The Elite Practice Academy addresses both of these issues.

It truly is a one-of-a-kind platform. In fact, there is no other platform made specifically for dentists and their teams that offers this level of comprehensive support.

I built it out of necessity. It was exactly what I needed in order to shift my practice to a self-multiplying business—one that was not reliant on me, or a team of high-maintenance superstars, to deliver an excellent and consistent patience experience—regardless of inevitable turnover. Everyone has turnover. If you are set up for it, you will not notice it. If you are not, it causes havoc.

Learn more about this revolutionary new way to develop your team at www.ElitePracticeFormulaBook.com.

CHAPTER 10

DELIVER THE FAIRY TALE EXPERIENCE WITH *CONSISTENCY*

Now you know the value in carefully engineering every single step of your "fairy tale experience," and leaving nothing to chance.

Implementing this knowledge allows you to create a supercharged referral machine by delivering world-class service to your patients at every touch-point of their visit. The result: they will have smiles on their faces as they walk through your hallways and sit in your chair. They will be grinning, and maybe even laughing, when they exit your door. Most importantly, they will beam when boasting about your services to their friends, family, and co-workers.

BUT YOU CANNOT STOP THERE...

Consistency in the calibre of patient experience must remain equal at EVERY touch-point. This includes post-treatment service, communication between recall visits, and any other occasion when a patient is in contact with your practice.

In fact, it is paramount that your patients do not feel like their exceptional experience ends after they pay for their treatment. Cultivating long-term relationships with your patients is what really builds businesses over time.

When your patients know you are remembering them because you care—even after you have been paid—the value of your gestures are far more impactful. For example, making care calls after treatment, sending birthday and special occasion cards, and recognizing patient's special events extend far beyond what is expected of you. It sets you apart. Now you are more than just their dentist. You are someone who cares. This plants a seed that inevitably sprouts the desire to refer you to their friends.

The magic in all of this is when you dramatically decrease the number of people who leave your practice for good, while at the same time increasing referrals, you achieve a perfect growth scenario.

SYSTEMIZE THE FAIRY TALE

What does sending patients cards have to do with employee training? They're two sides of the same coin. Both are integral components of the patient experience blueprint; they're the most important facet of your business.

The vast majority of businesses do not invest in their customers' experiences. The vast majority of individuals do not do this either. But if you want your practice to achieve high levels of success, clearly engineered systems for training and customer experience are necessary. **Your patient experience blueprint must be rooted in systemization**.

That is exactly how companies like Disney and the Ritz Carlton are able to create and maintain such consistent experiences. And remember—it is the experience promise that has built both of those businesses.

SECTION 4
LEADERSHIP

CHAPTER 11

ADOPT A WINNING MINDSET

I'm not talking about rah-rah cheerleading; I mean a mindset built on the principles of success and wealth attraction. How often do you think of an idea that could have a true impact on your business or your personal life, and then talk yourself out of it? Failing to take meaningful action for the idea would also be in the same category.

Why does this happen?

Usually we have a great idea, and then, along the way from idea to implementation, we are bombarded with a million distractions. Random employee issues, the general tasks associated with running a business, family obligations, the news, the weather, and politics are just a few of the distractions we may experience during one given day.

The problem with allowing all of these distractions to occupy our minds is that they begin to form our "circle of influence." The great Jim Rohn said it best – "You are the average of the five people you spend the most time with." This rule applies to our thoughts as well. What you put into your mind influences your beliefs, which creates your behaviour, which, in turn, creates your results.

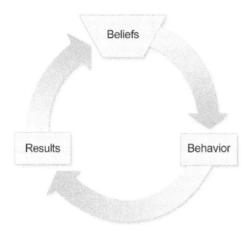

MINDSET MAKEOVER

If you want to change your results, you must change your beliefs; and therefore your thoughts and the information that influences them. This means you *MUST* pay attention to your circle of influence. Weed out all sources of information that do not align with your goals, especially those that negatively influence your thinking.

This does not mean you must stop speaking to anyone in particular, but you should consider limiting your exposure to negativity, and 'protecting your headspace.' After weeding out the negativity, you need to fill the now-empty space with empowering content, so other weeds don't see the unused area and take root. This entails installing a *USEFUL* mindset—one that is programmed for success.

It is often a realization for many that we even *have* a mindset – and that you can change it! Your mindset is like the operating system for your brain. It governs everything relating to your perception of the world around you.

FEEDING A POSITIVE MINDSET

To feed a positive and success-oriented mindset, you must actively avoid thinking and complaining about things you can't control. That means ignoring and not actively talking about the weather, the economy, taxes, politics, and so on.

In fact, we spend so much time obsessing over aspects of life we cannot control—and that, in the big picture, do not really matter—that we miss the sweet spot, a space from which we are able to operate most creatively and with the greatest impact.

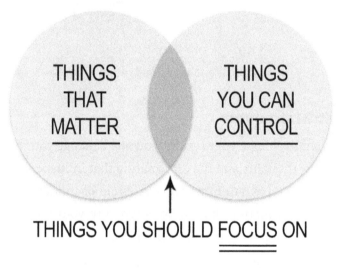

BELIEVE IT. ACHIEVE IT.

Napoleon Hill said, "Whatever the mind can conceive and believe, it can achieve."

This is not magic. It is grounded in science dating back to the 1960s, with Maxwell Maltz, a renowned psychologist, who showed that improving one's self-image can change the trajectory of their life.

If you truly want to transform your experience of success, take the time to clearly decide what you want your life to be like. Not some fantasy, but truly what you want from your business and personal life. The next step is to believe it is possible, and then act accordingly.

As you make changes aligned with your goals, avoid comparing yourself to others, as a measure of progress. Even if you are doing better than most, it only means you are better than average. If you really want to change your trajectory, compare yourself to your true potential. When potential becomes the standard, you will transform your business and life.

CHAPTER 12

NO CLEAR DIRECTION

The classic saying, 'If you don't know where you're going, any road will get you there,' couldn't be more true in the context of business.

Every dentist I know wants more new patients, more production, and more profit. Very few, however, have defined those items into detailed, manageable steps. A "fuzzy" goal cannot be achieved.

The first step toward goal achievement is to set a clearly-defined goal and write it down.

For example:

"I want more new patients," is a goal, but it lacks the criteria for success: measurability. All goals must be specific and measurable.

Instead, consider:

"I want to grow new patients from 40 per month to 70 per month, within 6 months."

This goal is actionable, which allows you to move forward.

The next step is to actually *take action*. This is where most people stop—an idea blooms in their minds, and it just dies there. The idea may return, it may tread water for a few moments, but will then get lost in the deep again.

One way to avoid goal die-off is to allow it to gain momentum. A simple momentum tool is writing your goal down and then placing it in a location you visit often, so you will be reminded of it throughout the day. Some great locations might include your bathroom mirror, or a conspicuous place on your desk.

An even more powerful practice is to hold an image of your goal, fully realized, in your mind. What are you doing when your goal has come to fruition? What does your life look like after you've achieved it? This practice actually allows you to harness the power of your mind, to spot and recognize opportunities relevant to achieving your goals when they cross your path.

If goal visualization sounds hokey, I can assure you it is grounded in science. The Reticular Activating Center in the brain (RAS) has the role of calling into your conscious mind any of the thousands of stimuli that your brain receives subconsciously at any given time. How does the RAS determine what is important? It can actually be programmed to prioritize certain stimuli, based on your thoughts. For example, holding a thought in your mind, such as "I am an excellent public speaker," will actually make you feel calmer, and improve your speaking over time— because your mind is open to ideas, methods, and techniques that you come across to make you a better speaker. This is the foundation of sports psychology.

TAKING ACTION

Let's pretend you have incorporated the steps above. Now that your brain is operating in a success mindset and is receptive to tools and information that will help you achieve your goal, you will need to break the goal into steps. Then TAKE ACTION.

For Example:

You have a 2 million dollar practice, and you want to grow by $800,000. How do you do it? There are several ways, but let's start with the easiest: increase new patient numbers. If your revenue per new patient is $3,000, you would need 267 new patients, which is about 22 new patients per month.

This is a relatively simple target. How do you achieve it? This material would require another book exclusively dedicated to the subject. For brevity's sake, we'll cover the basics. After setting a specific, measurable goal, the next step is to set a realistic timeframe. I am guilty of wanting everything now, but this just creates additional stress. It will make you feel that you can't achieve your goal. Instead, determine what is a reasonable timeframe, and take action toward the goal every day.

What if you don't know where to start?

I understand the frustration of feeling overwhelmed. I felt completely stuck in my career early on, and it is not a pleasant feeling. It is, however, the result of isolation. There is immense value in studying success and following the advice of a coach, or someone who has achieved what you want to achieve.

Clarity in your direction = sanity. Sanity in business is priceless. To learn how I turned a small solo practice generating an industry-average revenue into a high-seven-figure business growing at 12X the industry average while spending less and less time treating patients, visit www. ElitePracticeFormulaBook.com.

CHAPTER 13

ACTIVELY GROWING THE BUSINESS CULTURE

There is one area that few business owners focus on, but it is actually the most important place to begin. That is the culture of your organization.

Culture drives your competitive advantage.

It also drives your PROFIT.

Gone are the days of a top-down command-to-perform culture. Winning companies build a culture that INSPIRES the behaviours that create more value through work. When employees are fully engaged, they have more physical energy, and more positive emotional capacity—the same goes for you as well!

Culture can also be used to uphold accountability – which is something every business owner wants, but few are able to achieve. The patient experience you offer is the result of a series of well-choreographed behaviours *by employees*. Creating the right cultural climate in your practice will have a game-changing effect on your results. Done incorrectly, it can make it impossible to realize your potential.

Revenue per employee is also very different in highly engaged workplaces vs. disengaged workplaces. For example, Apple and Google earn well over a million dollars per employee.[27]

There was a Gallup study done a few years ago that said 71% of employees are disengaged, but 17% are ACTIVELY disengaged.[29] That means they are actively working against you. This is when your people are giving patients the vibe that – or outright saying that - you should probably go get this done somewhere else... Doc so-and-so down the road is cheaper. Isn't that interesting? The study goes on to say that 75% of your employees will steal from you. It's a very eye-opening study.

This is what disengagement causes. There is a very deliberate system to address this, because it takes a entire team effort to crush disengagement.

According to the Harvard Business review: "Engaged employees **consistently outperform in all categories** from customer service to sales, and "a highly engaged workforce can increase innovation, productivity, and bottom-line performance while reducing costs related to hiring and retention in highly competitive talent markets."[30]

DEVELOPING STRONG LEADERSHIP

A poll of 2 million employees from 700 companies showed that longevity and productivity was directly related to their relationship with their immediate boss.[28] Team members may see you as one of their

The Six Leadership Styles (Goleman)

	Commanding	Visionary	Affiliative	Democratic	Pacesetting	Coaching
The leader's modus operandi	Demands immediate compliance	Mobilizes people toward a vision	Creates harmony and builds emotional bonds	Forges consensus through participation	Sets high standards for performance	Develops people for the future
The style in a phrase	"Do what I tell you"	"Come with me"	"People come first"	"What do you think?"	"Do as I do now"	"Try this"
Underlying emotional intelligence competencies	Drive to achieve, initiative, self-control	Self-confidence, empathy, change catalyst	Empathy, building relationships, communication	Collaboration, team leadership, communication	Conscientiousness, drive to achieve, initiative	Developing others, empathy, self-awareness
When the style works best	In a crisis, to kick start a turnaround, or with problem employees	When changes require a new vision, or when a clear direction is needed	To heal rifts in a team or to motivate people during stressful circumstances	To build buy-in or consensus, or to get input from valuable employees	To get quick results, form a highly motivated and competent	To help an employee improve performance or develop long-term strengths
Overall impact on climate	Negative	Most strongly positive	Positive	Positive	Negative	Positive

Source: Goleman, Daniel, 'Leadership That Gets Results', 2000

immediate bosses. Be a leader. Part of your role is to uphold the bar you set for your business, while another part is to be a perpetual student of leadership. This will be an invaluable skill throughout your lifetime.

The best leaders can move fluidly and STRATEGICALLY between the 6 styles of leadership. Being everyone's friend all the time could be seen as valuable, but if you can't step out of that role and require results from your employees, you will become a doormat.

Another factor that's critical to your ability to lead is Emotional Intelligence, or EI. The graphic below over-simplifies this complex topic, but does allow for a quick introduction:

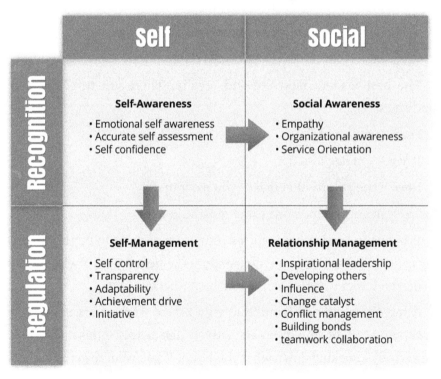

Emotional Intelligence

	Self	Social
Recognition	**Self-Awareness** • Emotional self awareness • Accurate self assessment • Self confidence	**Social Awareness** • Empathy • Organizational awareness • Service Orientation
Regulation	**Self-Management** • Self control • Transparency • Adaptability • Achievement drive • Initiative	**Relationship Management** • Inspirational leadership • Developing others • Influence • Change catalyst • Conflict management • Building bonds • teamwork collaboration

Growing your EI is paramount to growing your leadership skills, and therefore your business. The steps to doing so are:

1. Develop an awareness of yourself – define who you are, your values, and how you present yourself to others. You must be confident, but not arrogant.

2. Cultivate within yourself a drive to achieve.

3. Operate within the parameters of self-control, transparency, and the ability to adapt to changing circumstances.

4. Develop strong awareness of the world around you – including empathy for others and a service orientation.

5. Manage your relationships, by

   a. Being an inspirational leader,

   b. Developing and influencing others,

   c. Being a catalyst for change and managing conflict, and

   d. Building collaborative teamwork and bonds.

The best leaders motivate and inspire. There are three ways to motivate teams:

Fear – you *better* do

Duty – you *ought* to do

Love – the culture that makes you *want* to do

Can you guess which one is the most valuable?

When your leadership inspires your team to *want* to be thoroughly engaged in their work, tremendous value is achieved. This is why culture is such an integral component of business success.

A recent Gallup poll found that only 13% of workers are engaged at work, and 17.5% of employees are actively disengaged – this means they are actively knocking down what you build! If you want to get anywhere with your business, you must work on building a robust team culture.

Bottom line: engaged employees deliver results.

CHAPTER 14

LEVERAGE = FREEDOM

We are all *busy*, but are you *productive* with your days? Countless books and seminars have been created to help us eliminate the deluge of distractions that rob us of a non-renewable resource – *our time*. Distraction can come in many forms, like other people, or technology. We are busier than ever before, but also more distracted than ever before.

This distraction comes at a cost. Do you have unfinished projects, or goals that you just can't seem to achieve? I'll bet it's not for lack of trying. The problem lies in what we do with the time we have. Why are some people able to run three businesses and train for a marathon in a 24-hour day, while others are barely treading water, doing only half as much?

INTENTIONAL TIME MANAGEMENT

The strict discipline to be absolutely intentional with your time is the deciding factor between those who achieve high productivity levels and those who don't. For an in-depth look at these concepts, I'd recommend reading Dan Kennedy's *No B.S. Time Management for Entrepreneurs,* and Cal Newport's book, *Deep Work.* The basic principle outlined in these texts is if you want to accomplish something of value, you must dedicate blocks of time to this goal, during which you will be absolutely focused on getting that goal done— zero distractions, no exceptions.

It is remarkably effective. In fact, it is how I am able to run a thriving dental practice, a robust coaching program, two businesses unrelated to dentistry, publish books and reports, give presentations and seminars across North America, and still have time for my family.

LEVERAGE YOUR TIME THROUGH OTHERS

It's also important to remember that, no matter how savvy you become with your time, you are just one person. A natural extension of taking your own use of time seriously is *leveraging it through others*. As a busy entrepreneur-professional, this will become a necessity if you want to continue to increase your output, while maintaining or improving your personal life.

Every day you will find new areas in your business not running the way you want. For example, a new staff member may be performing a procedure their own way, and completely undoing the marketing and training you worked so hard to implement. It's a frustration that we as business owners know all too well. In between witnessing these catastrophic events, you are stopped 30 times an hour to answer the same question you have answered 100 times before. You start thinking, "If I'm seeing this much dysfunction, and I'm not by any means seeing all of it, who is going to go around, area by area, system by system, to *FIX THIS*?" It is impossible for you to do it all, because you are busy working *in the business*.

This is 'the battle' dentists, as small business owners, face. It is also the most energy-draining, morale-sucking part of your days.

Scaling up your business and establishing a leadership team offers a viable solution to this problem. Even if your leadership team is comprised of only one other person at first, you can still begin to offload some of your tasks that can be competently completed by others. This is the first step to strategically leveraging your time.

For most dentists, the establishment of time leverage can start with something as simple as your assistant making the temporary crown, so you can move on to the next patient. Essentially, you want to dissect your day, and remove all tasks that you could pay a $20-per-hour employee to do. This employee can do anything, from arranging travel and managing your calendar to picking up odd supplies, even groceries. Most of us can easily extract at least one more hour out of each day by delegating in this manner.

CREATING A LEADERSHIP TEAM

As your business grows, the next level of leveraging your time is building a true leadership team. This will be a group of people who typically oversee different departments. In clinical practice, this may be your dental assistant team leader, administrative team leader, hygiene team leader, and marketing director. You may have a site coordinator who oversees operations as well.

These positions are important in larger practices, because studies show that one person can only successfully oversee five people. After that, they lose control of the group. This is why you, as the doctor, cannot possibly run everything yourself.

Your role as the business owner is to establish the direction of your practice, and to align everyone with this vision. Your leadership team will then execute steps to ensure that everyone is following the systems you have established.

Of course, you do not want to make the delegating mistake that many business owners commit: giving a new employee a task to get something off your plate but failing to communicate the task at a level that they can accurately deliver the expected result. It is easy to understand why this happens. We are already busy and along comes a person who can help us - so we eagerly dump a bunch of tasks off our desk onto theirs. It seems counterintuitive that you must actually spend a much greater amount of time setting this person up for success on the front end, before they are ready to run and meet your expectations. Failing to do so often results in failure of the relationship. This is often the reason why so many practice owners never get to a point of leverage through others. They are too busy to stop and take the time to delegate properly, and therefore the person they delegate to ends up failing to deliver the desired result, and so they just end up doing it all themselves and never get out of that rut.

Instead, as we have discussed already, you must make a front-end effort to create a system, as well as clearly explain your "win conditions": the result from the system when done properly. You need to convey the best resulting scenario if a process is done correctly, as well as the worst scenario, if it is conducted incorrectly. This will allow your leadership team to embark on the right path toward achieving results, aligned with your vision for the business. This does take time to do, but once this is built, you won't have to repeat it. It can even be automated, as we will discuss later in this book.

You do not want to micromanage your leaders, but you do want to verify their results. Do this by asking for a specific and measurable result/statistic from each of them. Do this daily, or as often as you need, in order to verify that they are still within the guardrails of your vision. If a statistic gets out of range, you can have the leader give you the reasons, and their plan to improve or correct it.

Creating this level of accountability is like establishing a strong defensive line on a football team. Once you have drawn your line in the sand, their job is to make sure you are moving forward, and not giving up any ground.

When you do not have this level of accountability, the tail wags the dog. This is when the doctor (or a consultant) delivers a new direction that will better the business, but reaps limited results. This is primarily due to the fact that most people are naturally resistant to change. Consequently, a little pushback to the new changes occurs daily, until the new direction is either abandoned, or only minimally implemented. The doctor never achieves the desired new developments, because it is one person against a team of people, who would rather just keep doing what they are doing.

Having a solid and responsive leadership team, on the other hand, allows you to move mountains. For example, many of us are driven and motivated individuals – you have to be to make it through professional school. We are used to setting goals and achieving them. Think, however: how much more you could achieve if you had four other people, who also set goals every quarter and achieve them?

Once you reach the level of having a strong leadership team operating in your practice, you will need to become a serious student of leadership. People are not natural-born leaders – it is an acquired skill, and one very much worth pursuing. There are many books on the subject, and my recommendation is that you start reading as much as you can. It will be a long-term pursuit, but learning to lead and develop people will most certainly change the trajectory of your business.

CHAPTER 15

WHY YOUR PEOPLE WILL FOLLOW YOU

"If your actions inspire others to dream more, learn more, do more, and become more, you are a leader."

John Quincy Adams

MASTERING THE BUY-IN

One of the most valuable and important facets of leadership is buy-in: the ability to align people's thoughts, feelings, and actions with your vision. In order to persuade your employees to do what you ask of them, as opposed to what they want to do, they must believe in your vision. They must *buy-in* to your ideas. Furthermore, if you want to rally your team in a specific direction, they must be united around a *common purpose*. To be the most effective, that purpose has to be *bigger than themselves.*

YOU'RE A LEADER

You are a leader. Whether you realize it or not, your team looks up to you. You have influence over them. This isn't just because you pay them. They're following you because they're united around a common purpose they believe in: the impact of your business on the world around you.

Any time you initiate a change, your team will be looking at you, every step of the way. The second they witness a hint of disengagement from you, or that you aren't fully invested in the plan, they will push back. You will then lose ground.

Your mission is to keep the purpose of your vision at the forefront of your practice. Every day you need to remind your team (in various ways) the important reasons *why* "We do what we do," and why "We must continue to work on our game."

One exercise that I highly recommend is having everyone on your team participate in drawing a diagram that illustrates all of the areas that you and your team can make an impact in your world. It is a summary of your 'reasons why'—why you are making changes, and why you are pushing for progress. Here is an example of what my team came up with:

After drawing the diagram, spend some time digging deeper. Discuss how you and your team can impact your patients, fellow team members, and the community. Talk about how you may a have positive impact on the profession as well. It is vital that your team understands that the direction in which you want to lead them *is not about lining your pockets*. That is a side benefit, but there must be more to your vision than money—even for you. Money is a short-term high, but creating a real and lasting positive impact is what creates strong dedication.

For example, you could choose, as my team did, to positively impact your patients and community, and commit to a mission to CHANGE THE FACE OF DENTISTRY. These are large goals that can't be achieved by one single person. Their fruition relies on an entire team, working toward the same goal.

Once the goals are established, your job will be to motivate and lead your team daily. This begins with your morning huddle routine, which should be structured to ensure your team starts every day on a high. Effective morning huddles are particularly vital when introducing significant changes, like higher levels of systematization, or increased training. In my own practice, we have developed a system to create high-energy morning huddles. We even have a system that engages employees who aren't able to attend a huddle. You can learn more about all of these systems at www.ElitePracticeFormulaBook.com.

INCORPORATE LASTING CHANGE THROUGH HIGH-IMPACT LEADERSHIP

Change must be introduced through a consistent series of small steps, using 'buy-in' at every juncture. Anyone who works out or plays a sport understands the powerful role that consistent daily action plays in successful habit creation.

Perhaps the most simplistic book ever written on the subject is *Who Moved My Cheese?* by Spencer Johnson. It is a short read that conveys the power of accepting change. It aptly illustrates the fact that change is inevitable and required—not only for survival, but for growth.

The mental component of change can't be emphasized enough. Often we are trying to break through self-imposed limits—our own or those of our team – in order to grow. Self-imposed limits are very tenacious and, of course, originate in the mind. To the individuals possessing them, though, they ARE real, and completely justified. This is why you need to avoid taking the authoritative approach when trying to change a group. This approach only fuels resistance.

For this reason, we always introduce change beginning with WHY we must change. There is a great TED talk by Simon Sinek about starting with 'why.' According to Sinek, "People do not buy what we do, they buy WHY we do it." Starting with 'why' is critical in the beginning of the change process. As a leader, if you get this right, everything else will fall into place.

Furthermore, change begins at the top. Change is unsettling for people at all levels in a business, and when it is on the horizon, all eyes will turn to the leader/owner. That's you. The leader must embrace the new changes first, and then the ranks will follow.

You must have unwavering commitment to the change. This is high-impact leadership.

The Road to Change

The road to change is never perfect, but these steps will help keep the bumps to a minimum. Don't give up when you receive a little push-back from your team. It's just like raising a child; the boundaries will be tested. I'm reminded of the quote by Osman Minkara: "If you quit—quitting will become easier and easier for the rest of your life." This is true for your team as well.

It will be necessary to have conversations with individuals who are having difficulty with the change. Be supportive, but don't waver from the direction of change—encourage these employees. Tell them that they CAN do what they need to do, reinforce the reasons WHY, and hold the line. It takes patience and a little time, but when your team sees you are serious about change, it will happen.

Change might seem simple on the surface, and you might find yourself wondering as I often did, "Why won't this person just do what I ask?". Turns out, there is a deeper reason why people resist change than what you see on the surface. You are not simply asking for a different behavior; in many cases you are asking people to change *who they are* relative to their life at work. This is not a small request.

For example, if Sally has been working at your front desk for 10 years, and has always been the "go-to" person for the rest of the team when they have questions about anything administrative, when you ask Sally to change a great deal of "her way" of doing things, it is not just a new way of doing things - she is now on the same level as everyone else, and is not the "go-to" person anymore. This creates an internal resistance that is difficult to break through. This is the reason why you must begin any new training with the reason WHY it is so important, and how everyone will benefit from the change.

SECTION 5

MARKETING

CHAPTER 16

GET OUT OF THE BUSINESS OF DENTISTRY

THE KEY TO YOUR SUCCESS

Marketing, done the right way, is the key to achieving your ideal business outcome. In fact, it's the most important area upon which a business owner should focus.

As a dentist, if you do not promote your services, you cannot practice your profession.

Therefore, like it or not, you are not in the dental business—you are in the business of ***MARKETING DENTAL SERVICES.***

Done right, a ***strategic marketing plan*** will allow you to grow your practice into a business that supports the lifestyle you envisioned when you decided to become a dentist.

SMART MARKETING

Smart business owners know the difference between 'image branding' and direct response marketing. Image branding works for big corporations that can afford to splash their logos and taglines on a billboard or TV, just to keep their name in consumer's minds.

For small business owners, though, image branding is a bad idea. It offers a terrible return on investment, if return can be tracked at all.

Smart business owners also know that their marketing materials must have a 'call to action': an element that gets a prospective patient to raise their hand, and indicate their interest in your service.

Many business owners, however, make the mistake of using a lowest-price offer, instead of a strategic call to action. They're essentially giving away a service to get patients in the door. This may work, but the best businesses take a different, more rewarding approach.

The best businesses build Trusted Authority status in their market, and totally dominate the competition.

They do this by creating valuable content—and lots of it. Instead of offering free exams and deeply discounted services, they offer *information*. That information positions them as the expert in their area. Most people will go to an 'expert' over someone with the cheapest price. The trusted authority status also transcends commoditization pressures and can sustain your fees, even increase them.

The best businesses also understand that marketing is a complex web of interrelated processes that build on each other to keep prospective customers engaged, as well as to keep existing customers coming back.

BECOMING A TRUSTED AUTHORITY

To be the Trusted Authority in your market, you'll want to have:

1. A book
2. Special reports on each procedure you offer
3. Automated lead captures with weekly content emails to prospective and existing patients. This retains existing patients, and maintains the interest of prospective patients until they are ready to join your practice
4. Automated webinars on each procedure you offer
5. Live Seminars

6. Patient Events

7. A dominating social media presence, leveraging the key social media platforms

8. Domination of search engines and review sites

9. A patient-centric website

10. SEO

11. Blog posts

12. Press releases

13. Referral generation system

14. New patient welcome package and Email sequence

15. Original educational videos from you and your team

16. A monthly newsletter (shown to be a huge tool for retention and referrals)

17. A system of many internal marketing initiatives, like draws, contests, VIP nights, collection of testimonials and Google reviews, charitable initiatives, and many more

18. A clear initiative to have a tremendous positive impact in your community, so that you are seen as a generous community supporter. This furthers your Trusted Authority dominance.

I think you get the point: that marketing is clearly not giving your credit card to the newsletter companies or the website companies that come calling. It's a strategically-planned series of interrelated actions that result in referrals and new patients.

ALLOW THE SPOTLIGHT TO SHINE ON YOU

As you reach a Trusted Authority status, you must embrace the inevitable: people will begin to notice you. Many dentists are uncomfortable with this phenomenon. Many also resist the idea of marketing in general.

If you think that marketing is 'bad for the profession,' then let me ask you – how many people can you help, if no one knows you can help?

The reality of society today is that everyone is incredibly distracted. Unless you actively and intentionally *tell people* what you can do to help them, you won't achieve your goals for growth. What have you accomplished with your many years in school and your desire to help others, if patients never walk through your doors?

According to Sally Hogshead in her book, *Fascinate: Your 7 Triggers to Persuasion and Captivation*, there is a series of interactions that must occur for your patients to trust you. It starts with getting their attention. This is followed by capturing their interest and fascination—then, most importantly, their involvement in your world. This process leads to familiarity, and ultimately TRUST. **No trust = no relationship, no case acceptance, and no loyalty. This is a recipe for failure.**

BUILDING TRUST IS CRITICAL TO YOUR SUCCESS.

So, if familiarity builds trust, then it is only logical that being present in the lives of your patients, and active in your community, are the ultimate business builders.

How can you do this?

» Be generous with your time and money

» Found or participate in a community charity

» Host events for your patients and the community at large

» Be the source for information on all things dental

» And so on...

These actions will attract attention, but if you are doing them from a genuine desire to achieve the greatest positive impact through your work, why should anyone make you feel badly about it?

Never let the opinion of others be the yardstick by which you measure yourself.

CHAPTER 17

LEARN HOW TO FISH

If I could give you one gift, it would be to teach you how to think about marketing from a new, empowered position. This would make it so you aren't at the mercy of every sales representative who comes calling with the newest bright and shiny object, promising to erase all your practice worries. Usually these shiny objects address only one small area of your practice marketing. They also often cannot be tracked, which makes it difficult to determine if you are getting a positive return or just throwing money away.

Here is what the Elite Practice Marketing Strategy involves:

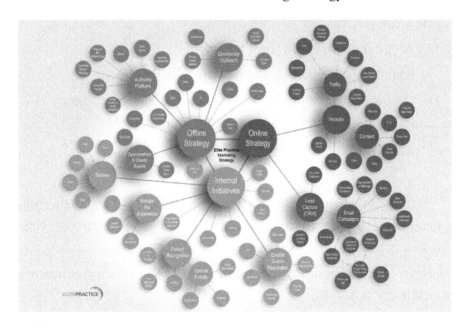

On the surface, it looks intimidating. So does climbing Mount Kilimanjaro.

There are no unreasonable goals; only unreasonable timeframes.

Let's look at the example of setting a goal to climb Mount Kilimanjaro. Most people would not start out by saying, "Okay, I'll start training today, and for the next seven days straight." If you actually wanted to accomplish this goal, you would start with the end result, and reverse-engineer a road to get there. You would break your process into small pieces that were manageable. You would figure out where to start, do your research, find out who to learn from, and ask about their experiences as well.

If you start out thinking this is impossible, then you are starting with the wrong mindset and the wrong mentors. In fact, the most valuable mentor in this example would be someone who tried to climb Mount Kilimanjaro and failed before eventually succeeding. There is great learning potential in the failures of others, and not just in studying their success stories.

I have mastered this marketing strategy mind map, as you see it here, and have broken it down into individual steps to take. You can learn more about this entire strategy at www.ElitePracticeFormulaBook.com.

If you want to climb a mountain, or you want to create authority in your business market, you need to align yourself with a mentor who can walk you through a complete strategy over time. You will also want to adjust your timeframe, because success in business is a long-term game.

CHAPTER 18

THEY'LL BREAK YOUR DOOR DOWN IF YOU LEARN THIS

I want you to think about **what your life would be like if you could double your business.** Could you take a few weeks of vacation? Spend a little more time with the kids? Finally go to bed without worrying about the future of your practice?

If you don't think it's possible, I'm going to challenge that right now. I have doubled my practice from the starting point of $200,000 per year **5 TIMES over an 8-year period**. Each time, I didn't think, going in, that it was possible.

CRUNCHING THE NUMBERS

This process begins by asking the right questions. The first question focuses on logistics. What will my business look like if I double it? How much revenue would we bring in each month? Each year? What is the current average value of a patient in our practice?

Using these questions, you can figure out how you can double your business.

Let's run through the numbers.

Let's take an average practice with a 1.2 million gross that treats an average 25 new patients per month (300 per year).

Average patient value (revenue per new patient) can be roughly calculated at 1,200,000/300 = $4,000.

If you want to add another 1.2 million in gross, then you need to add another 300 new patients per year ($4,000 x 300 = $1,200,000).

It is actually quite possible to do this over one year. But let's say you want to be more aggressive and go bigger though. You decide you want to set a two year goal. In year one, you want to add 450 new patients. In year two, you want to add 600.

Feeling overwhelmed? **Break the process down into a function of marketing.** If you are spending $10,000 per month total, in order to get the 25 new patients you are getting now, then your acquisition cost (cost of acquiring a new patient) is $10,000/25 = $400.

Consequently, if you want to reach 450 new patients in year one, you will be looking at spending $15,000 per month. During year two, you will need to spend $20,000, to bring in those new patients. This is a rough estimate, but, in my experience, this formula has been a reliable and easy way to **forecast marketing costs to reach a desired outcome.**

Of course, there is more to meeting growth goals than just spending a greater amount of money on marketing.

You must attract customers the right way. There is a stark difference between 'image' or 'branding' advertisements and direct response marketing. As we've discussed, image branding is for big corporations, with limitless advertising budgets. They can afford to spend millions on flashy print ads in trendy magazines, or to be on prime time TV.

Conversely, we are small business owners, and every dollar must be held accountable—if we send out a dollar, we want it to bring back two or three or more.

MARKETING FOR PROFESSIONALS IS NOT PROFESSIONAL

Let's take a moment to address the idea that marketing for professionals is not professional. Frankly, that idea died twenty years ago. The go-to method for your success is direct response marketing. If direct response marketing turns you off, remember, in today's economy, if you do not promote your business and stand out to highly distracted consumers, your business will not survive.

All direct response marketing pieces—whether applied to your website, a Facebook post, a postcard, or a newsletter—must have a few key elements:

1. Why patients should visit your practice, as opposed to every other option, including *doing nothing at all.*

2. An attention-grabbing headline that gets the recipient to actually read the piece. (People really do sort their mail over the wastebasket—if you don't make the "A" pile, you never get a chance to impress your potential patient!)

3. Compelling reasons why the prospective patient should take advantage of your services, with an emphasis on the benefit (particularly the emotional benefit) to them.

4. A call to action—a clearly-defined next step: "Call now," "Go to this website," etc.

You also need to utilize multiple media platforms and strategies to get your message out. These include your website, testimonials (used appropriately/legally), social media, video, direct mail, newsletters, Email, and so on.

MAKE IT INTERESTING

Your advertising must be compelling. When you are driving by the scene of an accident, for example, you always slow down and look—everyone does. This usually results in long lines and slowdowns on the highway, but the scene is so compelling that you *have to look*. That is the effect you must create with your advertising.

Here's a sample postcard that consistently generates five new patients, which we can turn into twenty with our internal marketing and patient experience. Let's say for the sake of this example, though, that we only count the immediate return of five new patients. Average revenue per new patient in my practice is $3,500. Therefore, five patients X $3,500 = $17,500 return on 10,000 pieces mailed. If a mailing costs us $2,821.00, **the ROI is at least 6 to 1 (a 520% return) - a great deal.** If you had a machine that you could put a dollar in and get 6 dollars back, how long would you stand there and put dollars in?

This is the power of direct response marketing.

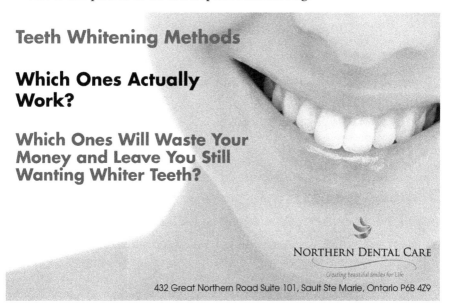

Teeth Whitening Methods

Which Ones Actually Work?

Which Ones Will Waste Your Money and Leave You Still Wanting Whiter Teeth?

NORTHERN DENTAL CARE

Creating Beautiful Smiles for Life

432 Great Northern Road Suite 101, Sault Ste Marie, Ontario P6B 4Z9

YET, THERE IS MORE...

The day you get a new patient is the day they start trying to leave. Why? They are being swayed in several directions, by countless advertisements. This includes buying the latest technological gadget and ignoring their dental needs.

Consequently, ***it's paramount that you have a strong strategy established to RETAIN your patients. According to the Harvard business review, 50% of customers in ANY business will leave every 5 years for a variety of reasons. You must have a strategy in place to keep them.***

We spend far too much time and money trying to attract new patients when our existing patients are an exceedingly better source of business and higher ROI. In fact, most dentists focus all their energy and marketing on new patients. Why spend 90% of your time, trying to convince total strangers to trust you with their health, when there's a rich, untapped market right under your nose?

This market knows you, trusts you, has the money to pay you, and wants you to succeed!

Think about it. If you're any good at what you do, and your personality isn't abusive, you should have no trouble re-marketing to existing patients.

It's relatively easy to make a sale to past patients, because they've already trusted you enough to give you their money at least once. Plus, the cost of acquisition is zero, because you know where to find them.

Have you ever determined what it costs you to acquire a new patient? It is worth doing the math on this—and quarterly, at the least. Simply take your total marketing spend and divide by the number of new patients. For a practice spending $10,000 per month/$120,000 per year on marketing and generating 200 new patients per year, it looks something like:

$120,000/200 = $600

So, if you are spending $600 to attract a new patient, what is your budget for keeping the ones you have? How much should it be? What strategies would work best?

As you just saw in the Elite Practice Marketing Strategy, the answer is complex; however, it is detailed in a step-by-step formula that can be replicated. For details visit www.ElitePracticeFormulaBook.com.

IT'S YOUR JOB TO STAND OUT

We are living in the most distracted society that has ever existed. Our work as marketers of dental services is to get noticed in a sea of sameness. (By the way, if you have not accepted that role, better accept it fast—your competition won't wait for you to catch up.)

CHAPTER 19

AUTOMATE YOUR MARKETING, MULTIPLY YOUR BUSINESS

Imagine, for a moment, that you're about to spend the day fishing, and you want to bring home A LOT of fish. Two options for your fishing experience lie before you. You could fish off of your little boat all day, using a nice rod and reel, or you could choose a commercial fishing boat, with a huge net spanning hundreds of metres. Which would you choose?

This sounds like an over-exaggeration, but it perfectly encapsulates the difference between marketing efforts employed by most dentists vs. what the top 1% of practices do.

My marketing platform is built on Infusionsoft—the leading CRM for small businesses. A CRM system will help you both close the gaps in your marketing systems and *automate repetitive marketing tasks,* to drive new patients to your practice on autopilot.

This offers tremendous value. It's the equivalent of adding additional full-time marketing staff to scale your marketing capacity, at will. It will make your office look like a well-run and sophisticated operation, allowing you to preempt your competition, because you are positioned as the obvious choice.

I've heard so many individuals say, "This won't work in professional practice/my business/my town," etc. If you have any doubts, I can prove to you that marketing automation works for ALL businesses—even bricks and mortar businesses like dentists—when incorporated into a proper strategy.

THE CUSTOMER LIFE CYCLE

Let's look closer at the customer lifecycle in any service business. Fundamentally, it looks like the diagram below. If you honestly and accurately assess how well your business addresses each of these areas, you will find the biggest opportunities for growth.

ATTRACT   CAPTURE LEADS   NURTURE PROSPECTS   DELIVER & WOW   GET REFERRALS   REPEAT

I know this seems like a lot of work. In fact, it is—if you are doing it all manually. Thankfully, great CRM software can be leveraged to automate much of this process.

YOUR IDEAL PATIENT

The first step to attracting patients to your practice is to determine who your ideal customer is—who is your buyer? For dentists, 90% of all appointments are made by women. Your target demographic is not the child, even if you see a lot of kids—it's mom. Knowing who you are trying to attract is your first priority.

Once this is established, you want to create ads that speak to your ideal prospect. Your goal is to literally join the conversation already taking place in their minds. For example, Mom doesn't want to take time off of work, or pull little Johnny out of school, in order to bring him to his dental appointment. Your ads need to address this want. Highlight your evening appointments and Saturday hours, so this problem is solved in your office.

Your ads should also be designed for use in various media, like direct mail, print, social media, Email, radio, etc. A well-written ad with compelling copies can be repurposed for all media. For a complete "Look-Over-My-Shoulder" study of the direct response strategy I use in my practice, visit www.ElitePracticeFormulaBook.com.

You also want to target your ads based on demographic information, like age, income, education, and psychographic information (behaviours, hobbies, and values).

The ads most successful at attracting leads offer no-obligation information, like free reports and e-books. Equally effective are contests and promotions, although not all jurisdictions allow these forms of advertising for professionals.

CAPTURE LEADS

The goal in this step is to get people to 'raise their hands,' and indicate that they're interested. Once they indicate interest, they will click on your ad, or go to your website. They will then be directed to a form with which they can trade their name and Email address for your information. If your information is compelling, they will want to make that exchange.

This is where automation begins to take over. If you have a great marketing piece that gets a lot of people to raise their hands, then you will have a high volume of people who want access to your information. If they called your office for this information, all you would be doing is answering the phone and mailing out free information nonstop. Instead, when a prospective patient fills out your online form, your CRM automatically sends out the requested free report, or other item, to their inbox. The software can do this an unlimited number of times, and at any speed necessary, for the volume your ads generate. You can even use this automation system to send out physical mail or packages without ever touching them.

NURTURE PROSPECTS

If I had a room full of people and asked everyone in the room, "Who is thinking of buying a car in the next 30 days?" a few hands would go up. If I asked who might buy a car in the next year, more hands would go up—and even more for the next three years.

The point is, when a prospective patient enters your ecosystem, you don't know at what stage she is currently in within the patient-lifecycle.

According to Business Insider[24], in order to enter the buyer's consciousness and make a significant penetration in a given market, you have to contact the prospect a minimum of seven times in an 18-month period.

Now, think about the people who call your admin employees and ask a question, but do not schedule. How many times do you call them back or follow-up with them over the next 18 months? Did you even get their names?

This is where the power of automation kicks in. By getting prospective patients to give you their names and Email addresses—at minimum—in exchange for the free answers to their questions via a free report online, you can now follow up with them indefinitely...until they become patients, or unsubscribe. If you are giving them great content, and are a conduit of great health information, they will stay with you.

To simplify the process, you can set up a campaign of follow-up Emails and great content to be sent automatically to prospective patients who have opted into your Email subscription. The key is to patiently and systematically motivate prospective patients to meet you—when they are ready. By doing this, you create familiarity, which eventually builds greater and greater trust in your brand.

DELIVER & WOW

Once a prospective patient has made the leap and scheduled a visit with your office, it's time to deliver the wow factor. Again, this can be automated. Once a patient becomes 'active' in your practice management software, your CRM can pick up that change, and send the new patient a welcome series of videos, or even physical letters or gifts.

GET REFERRALS

Once you and your team have delivered excellence, your software can then follow up with the patient. It can thank her for working with you, send her a congratulations letter on treatment completion, and even a survey, which can lead into asking for referrals.

Think about it—these are all common sense things that you *WANT* to happen with every patient, but in reality, they rarely do. Automation makes it just happen—on time, every time.

REPEAT

The next step in the automation process is to *systematically educate* your patients about everything you offer that may benefit them, or someone they know. Most of your customers will not realize the extent to which you can serve them. This reminds me of the story we all know too well: the patient who went and got veneers from the 'cosmetic dentist,' because they didn't think you did them.

You can avoid this frustration by automatically inserting your patients into a weekly campaign that highlights services you offer. The campaign should highlight them in interesting and entertaining ways. Over time, you'll find that such a campaign is great source of patient motivation. For example, a patient who wasn't really thinking about teeth whitening might come into your office for the procedure, after reading more about its benefits in one of your Emails.

A tremendous benefit of automation and CRM is their cost-effective nature. Email is inexpensive, and automation is far cheaper than a staff member. Even if you are sending physical packages or letters by mail through an automated system, you're still saving a lot of money. Perhaps the most expensive mistake is to miss these opportunities altogether.

Bottom line: a well-thought out marketing campaign will beat cold calling or image branding any day.

It also allows you to (as Dan Kennedy says), "Show up like nobody else." Your competitor isn't doing any of this. The result: you give the impression of an organized, sophisticated operation, even if you're a one-man show.

CHAPTER 20

WHERE AND WHAT TO INVEST

How Much Should I Spend?

My opinion on this question is extremely simple: spend as much as necessary to get the results you want. It should be a calculation based on the lifetime value of the patient. Until you know that number, you shouldn't be marketing.

The good news is that you can arrive at that number fairly quickly, with some rule-of-thumb estimates that are fairly reliable.

The easiest method for determining the lifetime value of the patient is to find your current acquisition cost and use it as a basis for future projections. To determine your acquisition cost, which is what you are currently spending to get a new patient, you simply divide the average monthly amount you are currently spending to get a new patient by the average number of new patients you actually get each month.

Let's say it costs you $150 to acquire a new patient. You now know that if you want to add 20 more new patients per month, you can expect to spend an additional $3,000 per month. Let's say your average annual revenue per patient is $3500. Your average patient remains with you for 5 years. So, your gross lifetime value of a new patient is $3500 x 5 = $17,500. Now this can fluctuate based on your profit margins and how many referrals you can stimulate. If you're operating at a 50% profit, each new patient is worth $8,750. If each patient refers you one new patient, their value goes up even more!

Forget percentages of production and all of that. You should be spending what is necessary. In fact, if you can, *outspend your competitors*. This strategy is guaranteed to grow your market share—provided, of course, that you have a tested and proven marketing strategy in place.

So, let's say you want to grow your practice by $1,000,000.

Here's how you would break it down:

Again, we'll assume your revenue per new patient is an average $3,500. This means that in order to get an additional $1,000,000 in revenue, you need 285 new patients. If your acquisition cost is $150 per patient, you will be spending at least an additional $42,750 in marketing. Of course, you could decrease that cost by increasing the number of referrals you get. (I'll get to that in just a moment).

While in a growth phase—which you are always in, if you are smart— you will be increasing your marketing spending every year. You will also be exceeding any industry norms for marketing expenses, as a certain percentage of production.

My marketing budget is significantly more than the 'industry norm.' Then again, the industry norm is a take-home of $150,000 per year. That is not true of my practice either. I don't want to be normal. You shouldn't either.

THE VALUE OF LIFETIME RELATIONSHIPS

It is of tremendous value to focus on nurturing lifetime relationships with your patients, because over time, the retention and referral base that results from this will allow you to decrease your acquisition cost.

Every patient that refers just one additional patient doubles his lifetime value. Promoting this habit among your patients is simply a matter of remaining in touch with them, and therefore nurturing a lifetime relationship. You can easily achieve this through automation, producing a monthly newsletter, hosting events, and internal initiatives.

Refer back to the diagram of the Elite Practice Marketing Strategy to help you on this front. As you can see, all parts are operating concurrently and synergistically. In reality, it will take some time to get there. Developing a comprehensive marketing strategy is one of the 4 pillars of success in the Elite Practice model.

ORCHESTRATE YOUR REFERRALS

When it comes to referrals, you want to orchestrate the process. Most people get referrals that are passive: an individual calls your office and says, "Hey, my brother was just in your office and said I should give you a call, because I'm having a problem with a back tooth." These referrals occur without you really doing anything to make them happen. Everyone receives these kinds of referrals.

The real opportunity for growth is in the orchestrated referral. It's truly the only type of referral that allows you to be in 100% control. An orchestrated referral is when you request and receive a specific kind of referral. For example, you may ask for a teeth-whitening referral from a patient, if that's a service you'd like to grow in your practice.

In order to employ the orchestrated referral method, a shift of mindset is necessary. You need to realize that the REAL reason patients refer is _not_ as a favor to you; they do it to make _themselves_ feel good.

This is a concept with which a lot of dentists and dental teams struggle. Most people are generally reluctant to ask for referrals, because, in their minds, they feel someone is doing _them_ a favor. When you have this mindset, it leads to reluctance. You don't want to be seen as _begging_ for business.

But in reality, people refer because _they want to feel good_—always.

When you've had a great experience, it's human nature to want to share that with others. We all do it—with restaurants, movies, books, and so on. If you know of something that's going to make another person happy—whether it's going to make them laugh, smile, provide some knowledge for their business, or give them a great experience—you want to share it, because it's how we're wired. It makes *us* feel good!

Your job is to leverage this fact toward the success of your practice. Give your patients tools to use as part of the process of orchestrating referrals. I give my patients copies of one of my books, called "Get Your Smile Back," so they may pass it on. My practice has also created a referral kit that patients are given to pass on to family, friends, and co-workers. Now all that's left in the growth equation is ensuring that they have a 'wow' experience. Your team and your internal systems will not have to take over and really over-deliver in service and experience for the patient to earn repeat business and referrals.

SECTION 6

PUTTING IT ALL TOGETHER

CHAPTER 21

YOUR IDEAL PRACTICE LIFE

Think, for a moment, about all of the things you like about the profession. Maybe you appreciate interacting with patients or team members or helping people get their smiles back, or perhaps you have a favorite procedure.

Now consider all the things that frustrate you about the profession.

I would bet that 99% of them have to do with running the business, and not the dentistry itself.

They're most likely responsibilities, such as hiring, training, managing operations, repairs to property, payroll, marketing, trying to balance these extra demands with patient treatment, and paying loans and mortgages—all while trying to find time for vacations and soccer games.

ESCAPING THE TRAP

How can you *leverage yourself,* so that you can build a *safety net* for sickness and afford to take time off, while maintaining or *increasing your income*?

What if you could multiply yourself, so that you did not have to be the sole provider of treatment? What if you could do all of this with a solid, recession-proof business model?

A multi-doctor clinic can provide the ultimate leverage, by enabling you to work less hours, create a safety net, take a vacation with the assurance that money is coming in, and allowing you to relax and enjoy your life more. Isn't this what you thought you were going to experience when you became a dentist?

Most solo practitioners *are* the business. They have no time left to work *on* the business.

The difficulty primarily materializes in the task of determining when and how to step off the treadmill.

Clarity on how to move forward will only come from gaining the business knowledge that can enable you to step out of the industry average and become one of the top 1% of dentists in the country. AND— **This can be done faster and easier than you could ever imagine.**

LIVING THE DREAM

Owning a multi-doctor clinic enables you to step into whatever role you want. You then become a business owner with the freedom of time and money to pursue other interests.

This model also allows you to have the greatest impact on your community and your team. It's a truly rewarding career, compared to the traditional solo practice model.

The biggest benefits for you:

1. **Less Stress**

2. **More Money**

3. **More Freedom**

A multi-doctor clinic also allows you to stay in tune with market trends, and deliver what patients actually want: longer hours of operation, along with evening and weekend appointments. Solo practitioners simply cannot accommodate this kind of schedule.

WEBINARS AND SEMINARS AREN'T THE ANSWER

If you're like most dentists, the concept of a multi-doctor clinic makes sense; however, it also seems logistically out of reach. You don't know where to start or how to manage it, and do not have a step-by-step process, to create clarity and confidence.

Webinars and seminars aren't the answer. During these events, a speaker tells you what needs to be done in each area of your business, and then leaves you on own to figure out how to implement the advice. This simply doesn't work.

How many webinars have you watched? How many seminars or training days have you attended? What was their impact? How much did you implement what was covered?

I have to ask you, honestly, to look in the mirror—and answer these questions:

How successful have you been in implementing business strategies?

How many new patients have you added to your practice, as a result of the advice offered in these webinars and weekend seminars?

By how much have they helped you increase your revenue?

How frustrated are you with the results?

A few of you may have taken some ideas and implemented them, but they probably took far too long to realize, and required far more effort than necessary.

Here's why they don't work:

1. **You are only getting a few little puzzle pieces during these events.**

2. You are struggling to implement them when you get home.

Maybe you learned how to improve your social media, or how to maximize your schedule—but these are just pieces of the greater puzzle, a drop in the bucket...

There are so many moving parts to growing every aspect of your business that you cannot cover everything in a weekend.

A ROADMAP TO SUCCESS

Imagine what you could do if you had a proven and tested model of success to copy.

Whether you choose to grow your practice as large as I have or not, there are some universal truths to success in business:

In order to build a strong business, in which you're not only surviving but thriving, you must have the three facets of a successful business working together, in synergy:

1. Operating your practice like a true business

2. Continuous team training on customer service and clinical systems alike

3. Marketing and promotion (with a very different approach)

For example, if you ramp up new patients, you must also improve your clinical efficiency to accommodate them.

If you improve the patient experience and overall level of customer service, you will also increase referrals. Your new patient flow is then multiplied by the experience your patients have.

Another important takeaway from what we've discussed is the principle of **leverage**. It's critical to energizing your entire business for success. You are already a busy doctor treating patients. You don't want to give up your personal time, **so the vast majority of your work should**

be automated. This means that systems and training are implemented, as well as new patients delivered, **without a heavy time commitment from you.**

The final important point: the most successful business owners invest in themselves, either through a private coach or a mastermind setting.

The reason is simple: **you can leapfrog over your competition by spending your time where it will be maximally impactful.** This is far more advantageous than learning from scratch, and trying to figure everything out on your own. Testing what works and what doesn't work is a costly method. Why not jump to the top of the pyramid, and learn how to do what you desire in your business, directly from those who have already successfully achieved it? **Simply put, you can copy success. You can save yourself time, money, and frustration—and even more importantly—REDUCE RISK!**

Maybe you want to be busier in your practice. Or perhaps, on the other end of the spectrum, you want to work less. You may even want move out of full-time practice, or stop practicing completely, to simply run the business.

There is a proven way to achieve each scenario. The smartest way to achieve your desired outcome is to align yourself with an expert who has realized your vision. They can show you exactly how they did it, and help you achieve your vision.

BECOME A SERIOUS STUDENT OF MARKETING OR PERISH

R.K. House and Associates, the company that compiles statistics for the Ontario Dental Association, recently said that **the 2025 fee guide will likely look almost identical to today's guide.** If you were disappointed about your lack of fee increase from last year, how do you feel about a zero fee increase for the next ten years? Somehow I don't think your overhead will have a zero increase over the next ten years.

Just consider inflation alone. How much of your income will you be forced to give up?

The ADA released some terrifying statistics as well in the past year—most notably the fact that **96% of dentists cannot afford to retire at age 65 and maintain their current lifestyle.**

There is serious downward pressure on fees by insurance companies, and outright bullying through their 'audits,' and attacks on well-intended professionals. The government, particularly in Ontario, is expecting dentists to serve the government-funded plans at 50-60% of current fees. They will do this by continuing to flood the market with foreign-trained dentists and setting up an environment favoring corporate consolidation, reducing our profession to a bunch of well-educated factory workers, who get to carry all the risk and stress of a business owner with the wage of anyone who has an average job.

Furthermore, the ever-increasing cost of equipment, supplies, and other expenses is **squeezing the solo practitioner in a way that is making solo practice a risky deal.**

AND—if you are like me and located in Canada - thanks to the new Canadian budget, you will now be paying up to 51% on your painfully-earned income!

STEPPING UP YOUR GAME

If you want to realize the dream you had when you went to professional school and invested seven or more years of your life—the income, lifestyle, and freedom you envisioned—then it's time to step up and make it happen.

Life does not reward whiners. **Life rewards those who TAKE ACTION.**

Yes, there is a big gap between the average dentist income of $150,000 and the top income earners, taking home more than 10 times that figure. An interesting point about this average that is often not considered on hearing the statistic is that in order to get a $150,000 average, many are taking home much less than that as well. For all the risk, stress, and level of education we all have, I believe this is simply NOT acceptable!

I'm here to tell you that YOU can be one of the top 1%.

All you need is the formula to get there, and an accountability partner. That's what I'm here for, **and I'm cheering for you to win.**

I want you to have the life you envisioned when you became a dentist. Let go of worrying about money or staff management, and step into the freedom to do what you want—when you want—without accumulating stress!

CHAPTER 22

FINAL COMMENTS

ARE YOU READY FOR A CHANGE?

Unless you're happy with the industry average of 10-15 new patients per month, something needs to change, and it's not your clinical skills.

Competition is heating up as the number of dentists continues to increase. Operational costs increase every year as well, but your fees do not. Consequently, you work harder and harder, yet never move forward. It's time to end this madness...

Once you become a practice owner, the dentistry becomes the easiest part of your day. You proceed to work what would be three full-time jobs in any other business: the primary producer, the leader/CEO, and the manager.

If you work 35-40 hours per week on patients, how much time can you spend working on the business? How effective can you be with that little amount of time? How much energy do you have left at the end of a clinical day?

Do you find yourself skipping activities you want to do, like spending time with your family, going to the gym, or just winding down—so you can put out fires in your practice? This doesn't have to be your life anymore. It's a choice, and it's yours.

INTENTIONAL ACTION

What steps are you willing to take NOW to change your current trajectory? Only significant change today can alter the direction in which you're headed. Don't be one of the 96% still hunched over a patient during their golden years, or being forced to 'settle' for a meager existence, after working so hard for so many years.

You are the CEO of your business. Become intentional in your actions. Plan and be held accountable, and you will realize your goals.

You need to get out of the business of trading hours for dollars and create some leverage. Even if you just want to practice dentistry and forget the headaches of running the business.

Whether you want to solely focus on practicing dentistry or step back into the business owner role, the process is simply a formula. It truly does take all systems firing together to create this type of practice. The good news is that it is POSSIBLE—with the right strategies and implementation methods.

In business, it always makes more sense to copy success, than to try to reinvent the wheel. I wasted hundreds of thousands of dollars on high-fee consultants, to only end up figuring out my own solutions in the end. I did glean some pearls of knowledge from every consultant, but was the one spreadsheet I still use worth the sixty grand?

THE RIGHT PATH

Let's say this all makes sense, and you realize you MUST close the gap with your business skills. What's next? Sure, you could begin an MBA program, spend $100,000, and invest two years of your life—but you're a practicing dentist, so that's out of the realm of possibility.

What about taking courses, and reading books? Certainly there is knowledge to be gained in this manner, but how much time can you truly devote to doing this? Which courses do you take? Which books do you read? How will you implement what you learn? *Will it work?*

The sheer volume of information available is daunting. No doubt, all necessary information is available for you to find, but how much time do you want to invest in this search? And how much money? How much frustration and disappointment can you take before you hit a wall?

And what about marketing? Do you know how to build yourself into a 'Trusted Authority'? Do you have the skillset to dominate your market, regardless of competition, without compromising your integrity?

STEPPING INTO FREEDOM

Would you be interested in learning a shortcut to the most impactful knowledge, skills, and systems for your practice? Would you like to learn a system that can be absolutely replicated by you?

There is one thing I have learned on my journey in the business world: the smart business owners and entrepreneurs *copy success.* There are no bonus points for spending hundreds of hours figuring things out the hard way. **The only thing that matters is the *result*!**

Consider the difference between the manner in which average 'mom and pop' restaurants set up their businesses, and the McDonald's Franchise method. The 'mom and pop' setup will establish their business cheaply, figure it out as they go, and will make around a $50,000 profit in a good year. The average McDonald's franchise is over one million dollars to set up, because you are buying the speed of systems and processes that can get a new restaurant from zero to six or seven figures in no time—with a bunch of teenagers working the operation to boot! This is the power of proven systems.

Don't waste another second. To DISCOVER the first and only legitimate, (proven in current practice), complete system for multiplying you practice income WHILE decreasing its day to day dependence on you, as chief day laborer and as overseer... for creating income certainty in an uncertain world....

Go to www.ElitePracticeFormulaBook.com and take the next step!

CITATIONS

1. http://www.ada.org/~/media/ADA/Member%20Center/FIles/ Escan2013_Diringer_Full.ashx

2. http://www.solutionreach.com/SERVICES/Patient-Retention

3. http://www.dentaleconomics.com/articles/print/volume-99/ issue-1/departments/flourishing-in-changing-times/percentage-of-overhead-is-a-choice.html

4. http://rcdso.org/PublicProtection/HowToFileAComplaint/Filea-Complaint

5. British Dental Journal 217, 269 - 270 (2014) Published online: 26 September 2014 | doi:10.1038/sj.bdj.2014.805 http://www.nature.com/bdj/journal/v217/n6/full/sj.bdj.2014.805.html

6. http://www.businessinsider.com/ap-facing-rising-dental-costs-seniors-head-to-mexico-2015-8

7. Australian Dental Journal 2005;50:(3):179-185 http://www.re-searchgate.net/publication/7528717_Job_satisfaction_of_registered_dental_practitioners

8. http://www.cbsnews.com/news/a-deadly-trip-to-the-dentist/ http://www.cbc.ca/news/canada/dentists-vary-widely-on-diagnosis-and-cost-cbc-marketplace-finds-1.1279371

9. https://www.youtube.com/watch?v=bIKsLleVsH8

10. https://adeachartingprogress.wordpress.com/2014/05/15/a-dentist-shortage-maybe-maybe-not/

11. https://hbr.org/1996/03/learning-from-customer-defections/ar/1

12. http://www.independent.co.uk/life-style/health-and-families/health-news/number-of-claims-against-dentists-has-quadrupled-774283.html

13. http://crushthedatexam.com/what-you-should-know-besfore-you-become-a-dentist/

14. http://solopreneur.ca/importance-of-vacation-time/

15. http://www.disabilitycanhappen.org/chances_disability/disability_stats.asp

16. http://returnonbehavior.com/2010/10/50-facts-about-customer-experience-for-2011/

17. http://www.skilledup.com/insights/how-top-companies-make-the-roi-case-for-employee-training

18. http://www.fastcompany.com/3028628/work-smart/infographic-how-much-a-bad-hire-will-actually-cost-you

19. http://brainworldmagazine.com/learning-memory-how-do-we-remember-and-why-do-we-often-forget/

20. http://www.lifehack.org/articles/productivity/you-will-remember-information-longer-you-hand-write-notes.html

21. https://www.td.org/Publications/Magazines/TD/TD-Archive/2014/11/2014-State-of-the-Industry-Report-Spending-on-Employee-Training-Remains-a-Priority

22. http://www.expertmagazine.com/EMOnline/RC/part2.htm

23. http://www.latimes.com/science/sciencenow/la-sci-sn-depression-among-medical-residents-20151208-story.html

24. http://www.gallup.com/poll/165269/worldwide-employees-engaged-work.aspx

25. http://www.cbsnews.com/news/employee-theft-are-you-blind-to-it/

26. http://www.businessinsider.com/how-many-contacts-does-it-take-before-someone-buys-your-product-2011-7

27.   http://www.businessinsider.com/top-tech-companies-reve-
       nue-per-employee-2015-10

28.   https://books.google.ca/books?id=5WCo4u_zoGQC&p-
       g=PA75&lpg=PA75&dq=2+million+employees+from+700+com-
       panies&source=bl&ots=cKOmOu3qGv&sig=pDyZQFQy46rf-
       v8DDYnwlpBJnhgs&hl=en&sa=X&ved=0ahUKEwjkxPao9ob-
       NAhUnEFIKHXwkAboQ6AEILDAD#v=onepage&q=2%20mil-
       lion%20employees%20from%20700%20companies&f=false

29.   http://www.gallup.com/poll/181289/majority-employ-
       ees-not-engaged-despite-gains-2014.aspx

30.   https://hbr.org/resources/pdfs/comm/achievers/hbr_achiev-
       ers_report_sep13.pdf

CPSIA information can be obtained
at www.ICGtesting.com
Printed in the USA
LVHW02s2236130318
569769LV00007B/9/P

9 781628 653816